English Skills 5

Answers

Carol Matchett

Schofield & Sims

Which book?

The **English Skills** books are aligned with the end-of-year objectives for Key Stage 2. For the majority of pupils aged seven to 11 years, follow the guidance given on page 2 as to which book to use with each year group.

If a pupil is working significantly above or below the standard normally expected for his or her age, another book may be more appropriate. If you are not sure which to choose, **Workbook descriptors** and a simple **Entry test** are available to help you identify the book that is best suited to the pupil's abilities. You can also use these resources with new pupils joining your class or school.

Photocopy masters of the **Workbook descriptors** and **Entry test** are provided in the **Teacher's Guide** – which also contains the **Entry test marking key**, full instructions for use, and a range of other **English Skills** copymasters. For ordering details, see page 46.

You may be using **English Skills** at Key Stage 3 or with other mixed-ability groups of young people or adults. In such cases you will find the **Workbook descriptors** and **Entry test** vital in deciding which book to give each student.

Published by Schofield & Sims Ltd,
Dogley Mill, Fenay Bridge, Huddersfield HD8 0NQ, UK
Telephone 01484 607080

www.schofieldandsims.co.uk

Author: Carol Matchett
Carol Matchett has asserted her moral right under the Copyright, Designs and Patents Act, 1988, to be identified as the author of this work.

British Library Cataloguing in Publication Data
A catalogue record for this book is available from the British Library.

Commissioning and editorial project management by
Carolyn Richardson Publishing Services *(www.publiserve.co.uk)*

*Design by **Ledgard Jepson Ltd***
*Printed in the UK by **Wyndeham Gait Ltd**, Grimsby, Lincolnshire*

Book 5 Answers ISBN 978 07217 1185 0

Contents

Schofield & Sims English Skills 5 Answers

SECTION 1

Spelling: Spelling unstressed vowels in polysyllabic words. Revising spelling rules (e.g., for adding vowel suffixes, doubling consonants, using **i** before **e**). Identifying and correcting common errors.

Word structure: Meaning and use of prefixes. Suffixes to change word classes (e.g., **tion**, **able**, **ible**). Common roots and their meanings.

Vocabulary: Words with everyday and subject-specific meanings. Technical words. Word formation (e.g., compounds, blends). Words no longer in regular use. Formal synonyms for connectives. Homophones; puns.

Sentence structure: Sentence construction for different text types; varying sentence length/type. Main/subordinate clauses; prepositional phrases; combining clauses. Embedding information. Active and passive.

Punctuation: Using apostrophes, speech marks, punctuation for effect, colons, dashes. Using commas and brackets for parenthesis.

Grammar: Words for specific purposes. Prepositions. Adverbials. Modifying nouns. Modal verbs. Point of view. Figurative language.

SECTION 2

Spelling: Using known words to spell unfamiliar words. Spelling rules and exceptions. Tricky letter strings/endings/graphemes; unstressed consonants. Anagrams. Mnemonics.

Word structure: Choosing the correct version of a suffix. Compound words (formal connectives e.g., **moreover**). Using root words for unstressed vowels.

Vocabulary: Words with multiple meanings. Changes in meaning over time; older/archaic vocabulary. Idioms, sayings, proverbs.

Sentence structure: Forming complex sentences; reordering clauses. Changing active to passive; using passives. Connectives. Conditional sentences.

Punctuation: Punctuating complex sentences. Using semi-colons.

Grammar: Word modifiers. Stylistic techniques. Verb tenses. Formal and informal language. Personification.

SECTION 3

Spelling: Correcting spelling. Using a dictionary. Spelling unfamiliar words.

Word structure: Words with related meanings and spellings.

Vocabulary: How writers from different times use language. Word derivations. Words with different meanings in different contexts.

Sentence structure: Varying sentence construction/length, for effect. Using passives to alter focus. Using conditionals to hypothesise.

Punctuation: Punctuating complex sentences to clarify meaning. Further use of the semi-colon.

Grammar: Language features of texts. Conveying meaning by implication. Word choice.

Teacher's notes

Introduction to the series

Schofield & Sims English Skills provides regular and carefully-graded practice in key literacy skills. It is designed for use alongside your existing literacy lessons, embedding key aspects of grammar, sentence structure, punctuation and spelling and constantly revisiting them until they become automatic. At the same time it reinforces and develops pupils' knowledge of word structure and vocabulary.

Each workbook comprises three sections with 12 tests in each one. The tests become more difficult, but the increase in difficulty is gradual. The workbooks are fully compatible with the Key Stage 2 literacy curriculum and the final tests in each book are aligned with the end-of-year objectives as follows:

- **Book 1:** Year 2
- **Book 2:** Year 3
- **Book 3:** Year 4
- **Book 4:** Year 5
- **Book 5:** Year 6
- **Book 6:** Years 6/7

Please note: Pupils working towards the objectives for an earlier year should use the appropriate workbook. There is no need for all members of the class to be working on the same book at the same time.

Parts A, B and C

Each test is divided into three parts:

- Part A: **Warm-up** – puzzles, 'warm-up' exercises and revision of earlier learning
- Part B: **Word work** – spelling, word structure, exploring words and their meanings
- Part C: **Sentence work** – putting words together to make sentences: for example, choosing suitable words, forming and punctuating sentences or checking for grammatical accuracy.

Answering the test questions

After you have demonstrated to the class how some of the different question types are to be answered, the pupils work through the test items without adult help – either individually or in pairs. For Books 2 to 6, encourage them to refer to dictionaries, thesauruses and other reference materials rather than asking for your help. The tests may be used flexibly. For example, a test may be tackled in one session or over several days.

Marking

This book provides correct answers for **English Skills 5**; where various different answers would be acceptable, an example is provided. The **Focus** panel stating the areas of learning being tested helps you to decide whether the pupil's answer is satisfactory. **Please note and explain to the class that if all or part of a question has several possible answers, the question number is displayed like this 5 . If a question has a specific answer, the question number is displayed like this 5 . It is displayed in this way even if the answer is made up of several parts that may be given in any order.**

Some questions test more than one area: for example, a question on writing in the past tense might also check pupils' knowledge of the spelling rules for adding **ed**. In such cases, both parts of the answer must be correct, reflecting real-life situations that require varied knowledge and skills.

Group marking sessions

Group or class marking sessions led by the teacher or classroom assistant are the most effective way of marking the tests: pupils learn by comparing and discussing answers.

Another benefit of group or class marking sessions is that they highlight deficits in pupils' knowledge, which will inform your future teaching. Where pupils have given a wrong answer, or none at all, briefly reinforce the key teaching point using an item from this book as a model. In a plenary discussion at the end of the session, encourage pupils to evaluate their own successes; each pupil can then work with a 'talk partner' to record areas needing improvement and discuss appropriate learning objectives.

Marking the end-of-section assessments

At the end of each workbook section are two writing assessments: the independent writing task and the proofreading task. These check that pupils are applying in their writing the knowledge, skills and understanding developed in the weekly tests. The assessments also provide evidence of a pupil's strengths and weaknesses, which will help you to set appropriate targets. You might consider sharing with the pupils a simplified version of the mark scheme – and then involve them in setting their own targets, as discussed above.

• *The independent writing task*

The independent writing task gives you a snapshot of a pupil's writing development. Prompts help pupils to plan and gather ideas so that when they begin writing they can focus on expressing their ideas clearly and effectively. On pages 16, 30 and 44 you will find photocopiable **Writing task assessment sheets** – one for each section – with specific assessment points arranged under the headings 'Sentence structure and punctuation', 'Composition and effect' and 'Spelling'. Complete one of these sheets as you mark each pupil's work.

• *The proofreading task*

The proofreading task focuses on punctuation, grammar and spelling. Examples of **Completed proofreading tasks** for each section, also photocopiable, are supplied on pages 17, 31 and 45. However, please note that pupils may choose to correct some of the errors using methods different to those shown in the example but equally valid. For example, two unpunctuated strings of words might be joined using a connective or separated to make two sentences. Additional evidence gained from the relevant proofreading task will help you to further assess pupils' achievements in 'Sentence punctuation' and 'Spelling' as already assessed in the writing task. If you wish, you can use the photocopiable sheet to make notes on a pupil's work.

Please note: Pupils whose scores against the assessment statements are low do not need to repeat a section. All the books revisit difficult areas and offer ample opportunities for further practice. Instead of holding a pupil back, highlight the assessment statements that reveal his or her weaknesses and use these to set learning targets. Ensure that pupils know their targets as they begin the next section.

Progress chart

On page 46 of the pupil workbook only you will find a **Progress chart**, with one column each for Sections 1, 2 and 3, and a list of 'I can' statements relating to the kinds of activities practised in the section. Please ask every pupil to complete the relevant column when they have finished working through a section.

The **Progress chart** encourages pupils to monitor their own work by identifying those activities that they have mastered and those requiring further attention. When pupils colour in the chart as recommended (**green** for **easy**, **orange** for **getting there** and **red** for **difficult**) it gives a clear picture of progress. It also shows the benefits of systematic practice: an activity that the pupil cannot perform in Section 1 later gets the 'green light'.

The **Progress chart** promotes assessment for learning and personalised learning. Whilst it is best completed in the workbook, so that achievements in all sections may be compared, you may at some point wish to have additional copies. For this reason, it may be photocopied. **However, all other pages of the pupil workbook remain strictly non-photocopiable.**

Section 1 Test 1

A WARM-UP

Write a sentence about computers.

1 In the past, <u>people mainly used computers at work.</u>

2 Today, <u>many people have computers at home.</u>

3 In the future, <u>children might have all their lessons on computers.</u>

Underline the word that is **not** correct.

4 decide recent <u>recult</u> recite decent

5 difference space advice <u>reverce</u> reduce

Write the antonym.

6 **inferior**   superior

7 **backhand**   forehand

8 **minor**   major

9 **exterior**   interior

10 **expansion** contraction

> **PART A Focus**
> **1–3:** past, present, future tense
> **4–5:** spelling words with soft c
> **6–10:** antonyms

B WORD WORK

1 Add the missing letters.

i e y

th_i_e f   m_y_st_e_ry

2 Write the plural forms of both words.

thieves   mysteries

3 Add the suffix **er** or **or**.

perform _er_   invent _or_   report _er_

4 Describe the words you have created.

Nouns naming people who carry out particular activities.

Write three more words of this type.

5 ending **er**: voyager, manager, jogger

6 ending **or**: creator, sailor, doctor

Write different definitions of each word.

7 **gear:** a set of wheels that work together inside a machine such as a car

8 **gear:** clothing, equipment

9 **coast** (verb): to cruise along

10 **coast** (noun): where land meets sea

> **PART B Focus**
> **1–2:** spelling strategies; plural rules
> **3–6:** suffixes; word classes
> **7–10:** words with two meanings; subject-specific words

C SENTENCE WORK

Add a prepositional phrase.

1 In the tunnel   , it was completely dark.

2 By seven o'clock   , it was completely dark.

3 At the edge of the forest   , the man turned and spoke.

4 Without warning   , the man turned and spoke.

> **PART C Focus**
> **1–4:** prepositional phrases at the start of a sentence
> **5–7:** precise vocabulary for impact
> **8–10:** punctuating direct speech

Cross out the three main verbs or verb phrases. Improve the sentence by writing new and more powerful verbs.

5 The RSPCA ~~asked~~ people to help as it ~~tried~~ to ~~cope with~~ the crisis. urged, struggled, manage

6 Residents ~~left~~ the meeting, ~~saying~~ that the situation had not been ~~sorted~~.
stormed out of, declaring, resolved

7 The wind ~~blew~~ through the trees, ~~breaking~~ branches and ~~throwing~~ them to the ground.
ripped, tearing off, hurling

Add punctuation and capital letters to these examples of direct speech.

8 Mrs Smith said, "It is very sad. We all feel let down."

9 "It's not fair," Mick complained. "I want to go with you."

10 Bill remembers the day well. "It was a bitterly cold morning," he explains.

A WARM-UP

Continue the sentence.

1 He stayed with Jen until _help came._

2 He stayed with Jen as long as _he dared._

_____

Make four words using these roots and affixes only.

trans port form er al

3	_transport_	**5**	_transform_
4	_porter_	**6**	_portal_

7 Add the same suffix to both words to make them into adjectives.

agree _able_   charge _able_

8 Add a different prefix to each of the words you have made. Write the new words.

disagreeable, rechargeable

Change one letter to make another onomatopoeia. Write the new word.

9 **chatter** _clatter_

10 **plod** _plop_

> **PART A Focus**
> **1–2:** using a range of connectives
> **3–8:** word structure
> **9–10:** onomatopoeia

B WORD WORK

Underline the word that is spelt correctly.

1 identifyed <u>identifying</u>

2 carryer <u>carrying</u>

3 <u>marrying</u> marryage

4 worryer <u>worrying</u>

5 Write the correct spelling of the words that were wrongly spelt.

identified, carrier, marriage, worrier

6 Add the correct '**shun**' ending.

techni _cian_   comple _tion_

posses _sion_   conclu _sion_

7 What kind of words have you made by adding the suffixes? Underline the correct answer.

verbs <u>nouns</u> adjectives

> **PART B Focus**
> **1–5:** adding vowel suffixes to words ending with y
> **6–7:** tion, sion and cian
> **8–10:** formal and informal synonyms

Write two more formal synonyms of the words in **bold**.

8 I'm **whacked**. _exhausted, drained_

9 It's a **phoney**. _a fake, a forgery_

10 We must **come clean**. _confess, admit it_

C SENTENCE WORK

Use one of these words to combine the two sentences. **that where who**

1 A theatre is a public building. Plays are performed there.

A theatre is a public building where plays are performed.

2 An orchestra is a group of musicians. They play many kinds of instruments.

An orchestra is a group of musicians who play many kinds of instruments.

3 A thermostat is a device on a heater. It controls the temperature.

A thermostat is a device on a heater that controls the temperature.

> **PART C Focus**
> **1–3:** combining sentences; connectives
> **4–6:** identifying uses of adverbs
> **7–10:** the possessive apostrophe with plurals

Underline the adverb and explain why the writer has used it.

4 She answered <u>wearily</u>. _It tells you how she answered, showing the character's feelings._

5 He is <u>very</u> clever. _It intensifies the adjective._

6 <u>Unfortunately</u>, City won 2–0. _It shows the writer's view of the events._

Complete the phrase by writing in an item or items belonging to the characters. Use the correct punctuation.

7 the pirates' _treasure_

8 the witches' _cauldron_

9 the gang's _hideaway_

10 the sheep's _pen_

Section 1 Test 3

A WARM-UP

Continue the sentence with a prepositional phrase.

1 Gus was left there _in the field._

_____

2 Gus was left there _throughout the night._

_____

3 Gus was left there _with his dog for_
company.

4 Continue the sentence using a conjunction.
Gus was left there _while the others_
searched the garden.

Add the same root to all three words.

5 _uni_ son   _uni_ corn   _uni_ cycle
6 _cent_ ury   _cent_ igrade   _cent_ ipede
7 _super_ nova   _super_ highway   _super_ power

Put the letters in order to make a word.

8 **g a r e l** _large_
9 **e r u s** _sure_
10 **l e t s y** _style_

> PART A Focus
> **1–4:** sentences using prepositional phrases; conjunctions
> **5–7:** common roots
> **8–10:** visual spelling strategies

B WORD WORK

The same syllable is missing from both words.
Write it in.

1 wid _en_ ing   threat _en_ ing
2 eas _i_ ly   laz _i_ ly
3 con _fer_ ence   re _fer_ ence

Split the word to show the root word and affixes.

4 overtaking   _over_ / _take_ / _ing_
5 regeneration   _re_ / _generate_ / _tion_
6 unbeneficial   _un_ / _benefit_ / _(c)ial_

Add a prefix and a suffix to make a new word.

7 _un_ control _lable_
8 _dis_ connect _ion_

> PART B Focus
> **1–3:** spelling unstressed vowels
> **4–8:** root words; affixes
> **9–10:** acronyms

Write in full the words that the letters stand for.

9 HQ   _headquarters_
10 ROM   _read only memory_

C SENTENCE WORK

Embed the information from the second sentence into the first. Write the new sentence.

> PART C Focus
> **1–3:** embedding information using commas or brackets
> **4–7:** shades of meaning; vocabulary for effect
> **8–10:** sentence punctuation

1 Michael helped David to escape. Michael is David's brother.
Michael, David's brother, helped him to escape.

2 Mrs Simmons raised £1000 for the charity. She works in a bank.
Mrs Simmons (who works in a bank) raised £1000 for the charity.

3 Ben won first prize. He is aged sixteen.   _Ben, aged sixteen, won first prize._

Sort the adjectives into two groups.   **calm cold rash sincere conceited fearless**

4 **positive:** _calm, fearless, sincere_   **5** **negative:** _cold, rash, conceited_

Cross out the words that sound negative. Write new words that are more positive.

6 ~~Peculiar~~ house for sale: ~~cramped~~ rooms and lots of ~~old~~ features.   _unique, cosy, original_

7 Lucy was so ~~nosy~~, with her ~~prying~~ eyes and constant ~~smirk~~.   _inquisitive, questioning, grin_

Add the missing full stops, commas and capital letters.

8 Aaron ran down the hill, shouting loudly. ~~t~~The dog, ignoring me, bounded after him.

9 After two difficult years, Marie, then aged ten, went to live with her grandmother.

10 The strangers came to a halt. Jessica looked up, pale and frightened.

6   X DEFINITIVE ANSWER   X SAMPLE ANSWER

Section 1   Test 4

A   WARM-UP

Write two adverbs which would show that a character is

1 sad: tearfully, forlornly

2 happy: joyfully, merrily

3 scared: nervously, timidly

Add the missing root.

Clue: to do with computers

4   inter active

5   hyper link

6   multi media

> **PART A Focus**
> 1–3: use of adverbs
> 4–7: common roots
> 8–10: word classes

7   Write one other word with each root.

intergalactic, hypermarket, multiple

Underline the odd one out.

8   possessive pronouns: ours its his <u>there's</u>

9   prepositions: with at during <u>an</u>

10 conjunctions: but if <u>all</u> until

B   WORD WORK

Add each suffix and write the new words.

ing ed ment

1   move   moving, moved, movement

2   involve   involving, involved, involvement

3   What spelling rule did you use?

Keep the 'e' if adding a consonant suffix.

Drop the 'e' if adding a vowel suffix.

Add one more word to each set.

> **PART B Focus**
> 1–3: adding suffixes; words ending with e
> 4–6: prefixes and their meanings
> 7–10: words with multiple meanings

4   predict prehistoric   previous

5   exit   exclude   expel

6   Write the meaning of the prefix.

pre: before   **ex:** out

Write four different definitions.

7   beat: the feel of the rhythm in music

8   beat: to whisk with a fork in cookery

9   beat: to defeat

10 beat: to strike or hit

C   SENTENCE WORK

Describe the technique that the writer has used in the title.

1   The Loch Ness monster – does it exist? The question intrigues the reader.

2   Save the whale – NOW! The imperative and capitals make it sound direct and urgent.

3   A simple solution? The question mark suggests that the solution might not be simple.

4   Use one of these techniques to write the title of an article on solar power.

Solar power – the way forward?

> **PART C Focus**
> 1–4: stylistic devices; punctuation for effect
> 5–7: modal verbs for precision
> 8–10: punctuating dialogue; reported speech

Rewrite the sentence so that it sounds less definite.

5   The ground will be ready on time.   The ground should be ready on time.

6   In the future we will all have electric cars.   In the future we might all have electric cars.

7   Michael used the key to escape.   Michael may have used the key to escape.

8   Rewrite this line from a playscript, using the correct punctuation and capital letters.

Olivia anxiously did you find it   Olivia (anxiously): Did you find it?

9   Rewrite the line as direct speech.   "Did you find it?" asked Olivia, anxiously.

10 Rewrite the line as reported speech.   Olivia asked if he had found it.

Section 1 Test 5

A WARM-UP

Use the words **cat** and **bowl** in

1 a sentence: _My cat will eat only from her bowl._

2 an imperative: _Give the cat a bowl of cold milk._

3 a question: _Where has the cat hidden its bowl?_

4 a rhyming couplet:

Maxi is a really funny cat

He hides his bowl under the mat.

weary polite tidy

Add the same suffix to each of the three words to make

5 nouns: _weariness, politeness, tidiness_

6 adverbs: _wearily, politely, tidily_

7 superlatives: _weariest, politest, tidiest_

Write a word using these letters. The letters must be used in this order.

8 r t n   _return_

9 d b l   _double_

10 p f m   _perform_

PART A Focus
1–4: sentence types; rhyming couplets
5–7: suffixes; word classes
8–10: visual spelling strategies

B WORD WORK

1 Add **ie** or **ei**.

p _ie_ c e   b r _ie_ f l y   r e c _ei_ p t

2 What rule did you use?

'i' before 'e' except after 'c'.

3 What do you notice about the spelling of these words?

weigh neigh eight height

They are all spelt 'ei', not 'ie'.

4 Write the word that sounds like the odd one out.

height

PART B Focus
1–4: when to apply i before e rule; exceptions
5–7: root words; word structure
8–10: subject-specific vocabulary

Write three words related to the word in **bold**.

5 hero   _heroism, heroic, superhero_

6 just   _justice, justly, injustice_

7 know   _Knowing, Knowledge, Known_

Write a definition. **_Clue: to do with plants_**

8 germination: _when a seed starts sprouting_

9 dispersal: _how seeds are scattered_

10 pollination: _how pollen is transferred_

C SENTENCE WORK

Identify the text type.

1 The brave teenager, now resting at home, rescued her trapped friends.   _newspaper report_

2 Hundreds of homeless animals are in urgent need of your help – right now.   _persuasive text_

3 The man with the white beard stood in the quiet, moonlit square.   _story_

Give two ways in which the nouns in sentences 1 to 3 are modified.

4 _Using expressive/descriptive adjectives._   **5** _Using prepositional phrases._

Write four words that could be used to complete the sentence.

6 He _____ be late today.   _could, might, will, may_

7 They _____ have passed us.   _may, will, must, could_

8 Put a tick if the apostrophes are used correctly. Put a cross if they are not.

Jenny's mum hadn't any money.   ✓   Fan's were eager to see Citys' new signing.   ✗

We could'nt hear the actor's dialogue.   ✗

Write correctly the sentences that you have put a cross beside.

9 _We couldn't hear the actors' dialogue._

10 _Fans were eager to see City's new signing._

PART C Focus
1–3: identifying text types
4–5: noun modification
6–7: modal verbs
8–10: using apostrophes

8

X DEFINITIVE ANSWER   X SAMPLE ANSWER

Section 1   Test 6

A   WARM-UP

Write an advertising slogan for a new snack
called choco-pops. Use

1 **rhyme:** Everything stops for choco-pops

2 **alliteration:** Cheery chirpy choco-pops

3 **word play:** They're chock-a-block with choc-o-late

4 **simile:** Choco-pops – like a chocolate explosion on your tongue

What word could you write in the gap to make
a new word? Write two possibilities.

5 dis_____ ly   order, honest

6 un _____ able   enjoy, touch

7 im _____ ion   press, perfect

Add the name of a drink to complete the word.

8 tea __ s e

9 cola __ n d e r

10 pop __ u l a r

> **PART A Focus**
> **1–4:** stylistic devices
> **5–7:** word structure
> **8–10:** spelling strategies; word play

B   WORD WORK

Cross out the words that are wrongly spelt.
Write the correct spelling.

1 To my ~~releif~~, the ~~queshuns~~ were not ~~difercult.~~
   relief, questions, difficult

2 The ~~worter~~ looked ~~inviteing,~~ she ~~thourt.~~
   water, inviting, thought

Add two words with the same ending.

3 **quarrelsome**   troublesome, fearsome

4 **toward**   downward, onward

5 **lengthwise**   clockwise, likewise

Draw a line to join the ending to its meaning.

6 **some** — in that way

7 **ward** — full of that quality

8 **wise** — in the given direction

> **PART B Focus**
> **1–2:** correcting common spelling errors
> **3–5:** word endings
> **6–8:** common roots and their meanings
> **9–10:** words with more than one meaning; word classes

Underline the words that

9 can be **nouns** as well as **adjectives:**
   ugly <u>annual</u> large <u>final</u> busy

10 can be **nouns** as well as **verbs:**
   <u>cook</u> rely <u>polish</u> deliver compose

C   SENTENCE WORK

Reorder the words to make three different sentences that sound better than the single sentence given.

The King saw the statue unfortunately as he entered the castle in the evening.

1 Unfortunately, the King saw the statue in the evening as he entered the castle.

2 As he entered the castle in the evening, unfortunately the King saw the statue.

3 In the evening, the King unfortunately saw the statue as he entered the castle.

She walked.

Write two adverbs or adverbial phrases that could be added to the sentence to say

4 **how:** slowly, purposefully

5 **where:** outside, here

6 **when:** a few days ago, at last

> **PART C Focus**
> **1–3:** reordering phrases, clauses, adverbs
> **4–6:** uses of adverbs
> **7–10:** brackets and commas for parenthesis

Add a pair of brackets within each sentence.

7 Some eagles build their nests (called eyries) on cliff tops.

8 Ned kept the two dogs (Shep and Flick) for many years.

9 Rob Jones (the team's manager) was unhappy with the decision.

10 What other punctuation could have been used instead of brackets?   A pair of commas or dashes.

A WARM-UP

Write a sentence using these words.

football cake

1 simple sentence: The football landed in the cake.

2 complex sentence: After playing football for an hour, we devoured the cake.

3 Draw a line to join the root to the suffix.

auto — mate
therm — ference
phon — ic
circum — al

> **PART A Focus**
> **1–2:** simple and complex sentences
> **3–7:** roots and their meanings
> **8–10:** compound words

Write the meaning of the root.

4 auto: self **6 phon:** sound

5 therm: heat **7 circum:** round

All these compound words are to do with computers. Complete them

8 using adjectives: short cut hard ware

9 using prepositions: down load on line

10 using nouns: task bar net work

B WORD WORK

1 Underline the root words.

   dangerous prosperous offering

2 Write each word split into syllables.

   dan / ger / ous   pros / per / ous

   of / fer / ing

3 Which letter is unstressed in all these words?

   the 'e'

Write the word to go with the definition.

Clue: starts with in or im

> **PART B Focus**
> **1–3:** spelling strategies; unstressed vowels
> **4–9:** word meanings; in and im prefixes
> **10:** shortened words

4 invisible : cannot be seen

5 incomplete : unfinished

6 immature : childish

7 immobile : fixed, cannot be moved

8 imperfect : faulty, flawed

9 inaccurate : wrong, not exact

10 Write the longer word that each word comes from.

fridge   refrigerator

panto   pantomime

flu   influenza

intercom   intercommunication system

C SENTENCE WORK

Underline the main clause.

1 He waited for hours despite the rain.

2 I enjoyed the game even though we lost.

Rewrite 1 and 2 above with the subordinate clause at the start.

3 Despite the rain, he waited for hours.

4 Even though we lost, I enjoyed the game.

Extend and improve the sentence to match the story genre.

5 A man went down the street. (fantasy)

The wizard sped down the street on his broomstick, weaving between the hovermobiles.

6 She heard footsteps. (traditional tale)

The girl had not gone far into the wood when she heard the patter of footsteps.

7 He saw a face. (horror)

Then, to his horror, he made out the twisted features of a hideous face.

Add a colon and continue the sentence.

> **PART C Focus**
> **1–4:** main and subordinate clauses
> **5–7:** fiction genre; style
> **8–10:** use of colon

8 An imperative is a command. For example: "Stand by the door!"

9 Abby checked her pockets: keys, pen, notebook and mobile phone.

10 For this trick you need a few simple objects: a hat, a rabbit and a magic wand.

X DEFINITIVE ANSWER   X SAMPLE ANSWER

Section 1 Test 8

A WARM-UP

Read the headline. Then write the first sentence of the article.

1 **United on cloud nine** _Melton United fans were ecstatic after their team's amazing 9-0 win over City._

2 **Thief caught red-handed** _A thief was arrested yesterday morning, still carrying the plant that he had stolen._

Write two words related to the word in **bold**.

3 **apology** _apologise, apologetic_

4 **mystery** _mysterious, mystify_

5 **apply** _application, reapply_

6 **calculate** _calculator, calculation_

7 Make six words using these roots and affixes only.

act view inter re er

review, viewer, interview, interact, react, reviewer

> **PART A Focus**
> **1–2:** meaning of idioms; introductory sentences
> **3–7:** root words; affixes
> **8–10:** spelling strategies

Add a short word to complete the longer word.

8 mea _sure_ ment   **10** ac _cord_ ingly

9 disap _point_ ed

B WORD WORK

Add suffixes to each root word to make three new words.

ing ed age er or able

1 stop _per_   stop _ping_   stop _page_

2 plan _ner_   plan _ned_   plan _ning_

3 edit _ing_   edit _able_   edit _or_

4 Which root word is unusual?

'edit', because you don't double the 't' before the suffix.

> **PART B Focus**
> **1–4:** double letter rule; exceptions
> **5–7:** prefixes; word meanings
> **8–10:** words with subject-specific meanings

Add the correct prefix.

5 The footballer signed a new _con_ tract.

6 I can _dis_ tract him while you escape.

7 Nothing will _de_ tract from her success.

Write a definition.

8 **pitch** (in music): _tone, high or low_

9 **pitch** (in sport): _an area for playing on_

10 **pitch** (in camping): _to put up a tent_

C SENTENCE WORK

Link the sentences in four different ways. You can change the order if you want to.

It was still snowing. Amy rushed outside. She made a snowman.

1 _While it was still snowing, Amy rushed outside and made a snowman._

2 _It was still snowing so Amy rushed outside and made a snowman._

3 _Amy rushed outside while it was still snowing to make a snowman._

4 _As Amy rushed outside to make a snowman, it was still snowing._

Write three alternatives for the word in **bold**. They do not have to be synonyms.

5 The man was **very** old. _quite, extremely, really_

6 The dog was **on** the table. _by, under, beside_

7 Write the name of the class of words that you used

in 5: _adverbs_   **in 6:** _prepositions_

> **PART C Focus**
> **1–4:** forming complex sentences
> **5–7:** word classes: adverbs and prepositions
> **8–10:** use of speech marks; quotations

Where might you use speech marks in a text of this type?

8 **in a newspaper report:** _around a direct quote – from a witness, for example_

9 **in a biography:** _around a quote from the person you are writing about_

10 **in a book review:** _around any examples taken directly from the text_

Section 1 Test 9

A WARM-UP

Reorder the words to make three different sentences.

was Stanley sat there beside her

1 There was Stanley, sat beside her.

2 There, sat beside her, was Stanley.

3 Sat beside her, there was Stanley.

Underline the possessive pronoun that is hidden in each word.

4 determined   5 profits

Underline the preposition that is hidden in each word.

6 money   7 recovery

Write an adverb using the word in **bold**.

8 **heart**   heartily

9 **fury**   furiously

10 Underline the word to which you can add **all** these prefixes.

re im dis

claim cover prove press

> **PART A Focus**
> 1–3: varying word order
> 4–7: word classes;
> visual spelling strategies
> 8–9: adverbs
> 10: prefixes; root words

B WORD WORK

Add the missing syllables.

1   ad / ven / ture
    Clue: exciting journey or series of events

2 ap / pre / hen / sive
    Clue: anxious

3 des / ti / na / tion
    Clue: where you are going to

4   il / lu / mi / nate
    Clue: light up

> **PART B Focus**
> 1–4: spelling strategies
> 5–7: root words; affixes
> 8–10: word structure; meanings

Write two words related to the word in **bold**.

5 **create**   creation, creativity

6 **vary**   variety, various

7 **image**   imagine, imaginary

Write a definition.
Clue: found in a book about the Moon

8 **weightlessness:** having no weight

9 **uninhabitable:** no-one can live there

10 **spherical:**   round like a ball

C SENTENCE WORK

Add the missing full stops, commas and capital letters.

1 Simon turned. It was the same voice. Yes, there was the mysterious stranger.

2 There was a crash. Stella jumped. She clutched the chair, waiting.

3 Underline the word that best describes how the text made you feel

in 1: excited calm scared   in 2: thrilled calm tense

> **PART C Focus**
> 1–4: punctuation for effect;
> stylistic effects
> 5–7: connectives
> 8–10: figurative language

4 How did the punctuation help create these effects? Short sentences create tension or excitement.

Write three connectives or connective phrases that could be used

5 **to show a result:** therefore, as a result, consequently

6 **to add more information:** also, furthermore, moreover

7 **to oppose:** however, whereas, in contrast

Continue the sentence with a simile or a metaphor that creates a feeling of

8 **panic:** The crowd moved like a huge animal fleeing from danger.

9 **calm:** The wind was a gentle giant softly rustling the trees.

10 **excitement:** The acrobat flew through the air like an arrow speeding to its target.

X DEFINITIVE ANSWER   X SAMPLE ANSWER

Section 1 Test 10

A WARM-UP

They found that the Tardis had disappeared.

Rewrite this sentence as

1 **an exclamation:** The Tardis had gone!

2 **a question:** What had happened to
the Tardis?

PART A Focus
1–3: sentence types; structures
4–6: word structure
7–10: root words

3 **a complex sentence:** As they raced
through the door, they realised that
the Tardis had disappeared.

The ending of the word is missing. Write two
suggestions as to what the complete word might be.

4 illu _____ illustrate, illuminate

5 imm _____ immense, immediate

6 intr _____ intricate, intrigue

Write two words related to the word in **bold**.

7 **perform** performer, performance

8 **drama** dramatic, dramatically

9 **idea** ideal, idealist

10 **assist** assistant, assistance

B WORD WORK

Add the same ending to all three words.

ery ary ory

1 diction ary   prim ary   ordin ary

2 flatt ery   lott ery   machin ery

3 categ ory   fact ory   hist ory

4 Make four words using these roots and
suffixes only.

PART B Focus
1–3: strategies for unstressed vowels
4–8: roots and their meanings
9–10: word formation; blends

graph auto bio y logy
autograph, biology,
autobiography, biography

Write the meaning of the root.

5 **auto:** self   **7** **bio:** life

6 **graph:** writing   **8** **logy:** the study of

9 Write a definition.

motel: a hotel for motorists

brunch: a late breakfast or early lunch

fanzine: a magazine for fans

10 How were all the words created?
By blending two existing words.

C SENTENCE WORK

Add a subordinate clause that gives a contrasting idea.

1 Some believe that the fire was caused deliberately whilst others say it was an accident.

2 Hannah was trembling while Kate stood over her, gloating.

3 They continued to struggle although their efforts were useless.

4 City had the better first half, whereas United were stronger in the second.

The subject is **Forest fires**. Write sentences on this subject for each of these text types.

5 **a newspaper report:** Last night, forest fires continued to rage in Southern Italy.

6 **an explanation:** Forest fires are common in many parts of the world.

7 **an imaginative description:** A single spark waited quietly, gathering its strength.

Add the missing apostrophes.

8 At six o'clock we're off to Jack's to watch City's replay.

9 I'm worried 'cause I don't think I'll be able to go to Marek's party.

10 It's Annie's idea but she says it won't work without my parents' help.

PART C Focus
1–4: adding subordinate clauses
5–7: text types: appropriate style; content
8–10: use of apostrophes

Section 1   Test 11

A   WARM-UP

1   Write a complex sentence using these words.

book   hair   pencil

As she was reading the book, she idly twisted her hair around the pencil.

Write four words with the ending **ture**.

First write two two-syllable words.

2   nature   **3**   capture

Now write two three-syllable words.

4   adventure   **5**   signature

Write two suffixes that you could add to all the words.

sharp   tight   bright   deep   light

6   en   **7**   ly

> **PART A Focus**
> **1**: forming complex sentences
> **2–5**: spelling patterns
> **6–7**: suffixes
> **8–10**: similes

Complete the simile.

8   As springy as   elastic legs.

9   As welcome as   the start of spring.

10   As silent as   a falling snowflake.

B   WORD WORK

Add the missing vowels.

1   l e m o n a d e

2   s i m i l a r

3   s k e l e t o n

4   b e n e f i t

> **PART B Focus**
> **1–4**: stressed and unstressed vowels
> **5–8**: suffixes; changing word classes
> **9–10**: older words

Write a noun related to the word in **bold**.

5   **survive**   survival

6   **science**   scientist

Write an adjective related to the word in **bold**.

7   **courage**   courageous

8   **construct**   constructive

These words are in a novel set in Victorian times. What do they mean?

9   **victuals:**   food

10   **comforter:**   scarf

C   SENTENCE WORK

Is the sentence active or passive? Write your answer.

1   The case was closed.   passive

2   A stranger opened the door.   active

3   Rain destroyed the crops.   active

> **PART C Focus**
> **1–5**: active and passive forms
> **6–8**: varying sentences for effect; juxtaposing long and short sentences
> **9–10**: sentence punctuation, including speech marks

Rewrite the active sentences as passive sentences.

4   The door was opened by a stranger.   **5**   The crops were destroyed by rain.

Continue the sentence so that it builds up suspense.

6   I followed the path   as it twisted through the sinister tangle of branches, right into the heart of the forest.

Write two short contrasting sentences to follow the long complex one that you have just written.

7   A twig snapped close by.   **8**   What was it?

Punctuate the extract.

9   Mr Gold remembers Ilford as it was. "My aunt's flat was above Wilson's dairy," he recalls.

10   Julia Hopkins, who judged the competition, said, "Nikki's poster is really eye-catching."

14 | X | DEFINITIVE ANSWER | X | SAMPLE ANSWER

Section 1   Test 12

A   WARM-UP

Write a pun based on the homophones.

1 hair/hare: Stray dog causes hare-raising experience.

2 right/write: Evening book launch – all write on the night.

3 sent/scent: A perfume that is heaven scent.

4 you/ewe: "It's all right for ewe," says cow to sheep outside burger bar.

Underline the words that

> **PART A Focus**
> 1–4: puns; homophones
> 5–7: unusual plurals
> 8–10: prefixes

5 do **not** have a plural form:

child <u>furniture</u> goose <u>advice</u>

6 do **not** have a singular form:

<u>trousers</u> wolves <u>binoculars</u> teeth

7 are the same whether singular or plural:

<u>sheep</u> mice patio <u>deer</u> solo

Add the same prefix to all three words.

8 <u>de</u> fault   <u>de</u> flate   <u>de</u> compose

9 <u>co</u> exist   <u>co</u> operate   <u>co</u> -star

10 <u>en</u> large   <u>en</u> grave   <u>en</u> trust

B   WORD WORK

Cross out the words that are wrongly spelt.
Write the correct spelling.

1 ~~consernant~~: a letter of the ~~alfabet~~ that is not a ~~vowle~~ consonant, alphabet, vowel

2 ~~ajective~~: a ~~werd~~ that ~~discribes~~ a ~~known~~ adjective, word, describes, noun

3 ~~simele~~: when a ~~writter~~ makes a ~~comperison~~ simile, writer, comparison

Write the root word and its meaning.

4 popular population populate

popu(lus)   means   people

5 pedal pedestrian pedometer

ped(is)   means   foot

6 aeroplane aerospace aerosol

aero   means   air

> **PART B Focus**
> 1–3: correcting common spelling errors
> 4–7: meaning of roots
> 8–10: synonyms for connectives

7 prime primary primrose

prim(a/us)   means   first

Write two synonyms.

8 also   additionally, moreover

9 so   consequently, therefore

10 next   after that, subsequently

C   SENTENCE WORK

Rewrite the sentence in the passive form.

1 City won the game.   The game was won by City.

2 The Mayor presented the prize.   The prize was presented by the Mayor.

3 Jaguar made the car in 1922.   The car was made by Jaguar in 1922.

4 The waves splashed the spectators.   The spectators were splashed by the waves.

The old lady glared at the boy standing by her gate.

> **PART C Focus**
> 1–4: changing active to passive
> 5–7: point of view; first and third person
> 8–10: punctuation for effect

5 Is the sentence in the first, second or third person?   third person

Rewrite and add more detail to the sentence from the point of view of

6 the woman: I glared at the young lad who loitered suspiciously by my gate.

7 the boy: The evil old woman gave me a filthy glare just for standing by her gate.

Punctuate the sentence so that it sounds effective.

8 They had no key and yet, as if by magic, slowly, so very slowly, the door opened.

9 Try them today–they're great!

10 What different effects have been created in these two sentences?

The commas in the first slow it down. The exclamation mark gives the second energy.

Schofield & Sims English Skills 5

Section 1 Writing task assessment sheet: The happening

Name	Class/Set
Teacher's name	Date

Sentence structure and punctuation

	Always/often	Sometimes	Never
Varies sentence length for contrast and effect (e.g., short for pace or impact; complex for description); embeds clauses for economy			
Uses adverbials, expanded phrases and clauses to add detail or suggest narrator's view			
Uses a variety of connectives to link ideas			
Uses verbs accurately; uses varied time references			
Sentences shaped for subtle effect/emphasis (e.g., delaying the focus of the sentence)			
Sentences demarcated correctly			
Direct speech set out on new line and demarcated with speech marks			
Commas (including parenthetic commas) used to mark phrases and clauses			
Uses apostrophes correctly			
Uses sophisticated punctuation (dash, colon, brackets)			

Composition and effect

	Always/often	Sometimes	Never
Character, setting and events are developed to match chosen genre and help make an impact			
Events shaped into paragraphs, which vary in length and structure			
Relationships between paragraphs made clear			
Narrative viewpoint (e.g., selection of detail, portrayal of actions) is controlled			
Techniques used to engage the reader (e.g., repetition, questions, direct address)			
Feelings, moods and attitudes expressed through stylistic devices (e.g., similes, metaphors)			
Apt vocabulary choices add to the impact			

Spelling

	Always/often	Sometimes	Never
High- and medium-frequency words and regular polysyllabic words are spelt correctly			
Words with unstressed vowels spelt correctly			
Common letter strings and endings correct			
Common roots, prefixes and suffixes (e.g., **tion**, **able**, **ible**) spelt correctly			
Rules for adding suffixes (e.g., **ed**, **ing**, **s**) and words ending with **e** applied correctly			

From: **English Skills 5 Answers** by Carol Matchett (ISBN 978 07217 1185 0). Copyright © Schofield & Sims Ltd, 2011. Published by Schofield & Sims Ltd, Dogley Mill, Fenay Bridge, Huddersfield HD8 0NQ, UK (www.schofieldandsims.co.uk). **This page may be photocopied for use within your school or institution only.**

Schofield & Sims English Skills 5

Section 1 Completed proofreading task: Flood!

Name	Class/Set
Teacher's name	Date

All day, worter levels have continewed to rise, threatning many locul home's.
(a = worter→a; e = levels→e; u = continewed→u; e = threatning; a = locul→a)

Mr Jackson, the cheef flood offiser, said, "of coarse people are feeling apprahensive, and we are offring addvise and asistence wearever posserble."
(i = cheef; c = offiser; O = of→O; u = coarse; e = apprahensive; e = offring; c = addvise; s a = asistence; h = wearever; i = posserble)

The floods have allso coursed caos for trannsport. earlyer on, the polise said that "it was dangrus to travul and peeple shoud stay put, as many drivers' cars were allready underwerter."
(au = coursed; h = caos; E i = earlyer; c = polise; eo = dangrus; e = travul; o = peeple; l = shoud; were = was→were; a = allready→underwerter a)

The Brown famerly, who live in the villije, told us "they could not beleive how quickerly the warter rows, but they were releeved to be safe."
(i = famerly; ag = villije; e = beleive; e = quickerly→rows e; i = releeved)

It seems peeple have no worning of the danjer, even thowgh their is a history of flooding in the locall erea.
(o = peeple; d = have→danjer d; a = worning; g = danjer; u = thowgh; e = their e; o = history; a = locall; a = erea)

Wether forcaster's are predictting more rain this everning – so it is posserble that there is werse to come.
(a = Wether; e e = forcaster's; e = predictting; u = everning; i = posserble; o = werse)

Section 1 tasks summary

Section 2　Test 1

A　WARM-UP

Rewrite the sentence, replacing some of the words with more interesting ones.

1　The woman gets out of the car.
The film star emerges from her limousine.

2　The dog looked at the man.
The bulldog peered at the postman.

3　The man came into the room.
The judge swept into court.

Add one letter to make a new word.

4　**smile**　*simile*
5　**cause**　*clause*
6　**phase**　*phrase*
7　**nun**　*noun*

Write two words related to the word in **bold**.

8　**destroy**　*destroyer, destruction*
9　**apply**　*reapply, application*
10　**equal**　*equality, equate*

B　WORD WORK

Part of each word is missing. Write in some letters to make a complete word.

1　script *ure*　pre script *ion*　manu script
2　verb *al*　ad verb *ial*　ad verb
3　part *icular*　im part *ial*　im part

Underline the correct spelling.

4　terrifyied <u>terrified</u> terryfed
5　hurryedly hurridly <u>hurriedly</u>
6　fancyful <u>fanciful</u> fancifull
7　<u>sunniest</u> sunnyest suniest

Write a definition of the word in **bold**.

8　the sea **bed**: *the bottom of the sea*

9　at the **crease**: *the batting or playing area (e.g., in cricket)*

10　a **litter** of three: *a family of baby animals*

C　SENTENCE WORK

Rewrite the information as a single complex sentence. Do so in two different ways.

Oxygen is a gas. It is found in the air. It is essential to life.

1　*Oxygen is a gas that is found in the air and is essential to life.*
2　*The gas oxygen, which is found in the air, is essential to life.*
3　Why do the complex sentences sound better? *They flow more effectively.*

Add a **prepositional phrase** to modify the noun and an **adverb** to modify the verb or adjective.

4　The cat *with one eye* sat *patiently* outside.
5　The man *from the corner shop* was not *really* amused.
6　The tree *at the end of the garden* was swaying *violently* .

One day almost five years later the man returned.

Punctuate the sentence using

7　**commas:** *One day, almost five years later, the man returned.*
8　**brackets:** *One day (almost five years later) the man returned.*
9　**dashes:** *One day – almost five years later – the man returned.*
10　What are the different effects of these punctuation marks? *Brackets and dashes cut off the information more definitely. Commas cause less of a break in the sentence.*

X DEFINITIVE ANSWER　　X SAMPLE ANSWER

Section 2   Test 2

A   WARM-UP

Add three adverbs to make a sentence that says **when**, **how** and **where**.

1 ___Yesterday___ it rained ___heavily everywhere___ .

2 ___Today___ we played ___happily outdoors___ .

3 The man ___always___ waits ___patiently outside___ .

Make a word that ends and a word that starts with each letter string.

4 ___compl___ ex → ex ___cel___

5 ___mer___ cy → cy ___cle___

6 ___dan___ ce → ce ___ntre___

PART A Focus
1–3: use of adverbs
4–6: letter strings; spelling strategies
7–10: homophones

Write a sentence using the homophones.

7 **bear/bare:** The bear's cupboard was bare.

8 **whale/wail:** The whale let out a wail.

9 **dear/deer:** "Oh dear," said the deer.

10 **hare/hair:** The old hare lost his hair.

B   WORD WORK

Add a suffix to make the word into a noun.

1 suspend ___sion___

2 alter ___ation___

Write a noun related to the word in **bold**. It should describe a person who

3 **tours:** ___tourist___

4 **assists:** ___assistant___

Add the missing syllables.

5 im / ___me___ / ___di___ / ___ate___ / ly
Clue: straightaway

6 ap / ___prox___ / ___i___ / ___mate___ / ly
Clue: roughly, about

7 ex / ___tra___ / ___or___ / ___din___ / ary
Clue: remarkable

PART B Focus
1–4: adding suffixes; word classes
5–7: spelling strategies
8–10: changes in word use

Write a modern word or phrase that means the same.

8 **wireless:** ___radio___

9 **primer:** ___school book___

10 **automobile:** ___car___

C   SENTENCE WORK

Complete the sentence using these words. **orange football**

1 Although ___the orange was large, (it was not as big as a football)___

2 After ___playing football for an hour, (they were glad of the orange juice)___

3 As ___it is the team's colour, (I wear an orange football scarf)___

4 Draw a ring round the main clause in each sentence.

PART C Focus
1–4: complex sentences; clauses
5–7: persuasive techniques
8–10: commas in sentences

You are writing an advert for a new brand of trainers. Write three techniques you might use, giving an example of each one.

5 rhetorical question: ___Are you fast enough?___

6 persuasive words: ___hi-tech, cool, the best on the block___

7 slogan: ___Beat the rest and be the best!___

Add two commas.

8 They plunged onwards, pushing deeper into the tunnel, losing all sense of direction.

9 Meanwhile, Sophie, sitting on the hillside, felt the land tremble beneath her.

10 Apes, unlike monkeys, have no tails.

Section 2 Test 3

A WARM-UP

Write a sentence using these words.

pigeon wall

1 simple sentence: _An enormous pigeon was sitting on the garden wall._

2 compound sentence: _The pigeon was sitting on the wall but then it flew away._

3 complex sentence: _I fell off the wall because I glimpsed an enormous pigeon._

Complete the mnemonic, which helps you to spell the word in **bold**.

4 You find a ___dent___ in an **acci** ___dent___ .

5 There is a ___rat___ in **sepa** ___rat___ e.

6 Poor old ___Al___ is in **hospit** ___al___ .

7 Find the p ___ie___ in p ___ie___ ces.

Write two words related to the word in **bold**.

8 **identity** _identify, identikit_

9 **belief** _believe, disbelief_

10 **human** _humane, humanity_

PART A Focus
1–3: varying sentence structures
4–7: spelling strategies; mnemonics
8–10: root words

B WORD WORK

Write the word to go with the definition.
The word begins with one of these prefixes.

PART B Focus
1–3: spelling words with prefixes; suffixes
4–6: i before e spelling rule; exceptions
7–10: sayings; proverbs

il im ir

1 _immortal_ : will never die

2 _illegal_ : against the law

3 _irreversible_ : cannot be changed back or undone

Add **ei** or **ie** to make the long **ee** sound.

4 d e c _ei_ t   y _ie_ l d   s _ei_ z e

5 r e l _ie_ v e   s _ie_ g e   w _ei_ r d

6 Which two words in questions 4 and 5 do **not** follow the normal 'i before e' rule?

'seize' and 'weird'

Complete the well-known saying.

7 All that glitters _is not gold._

8 The early bird _catches the worm._

9 There's no smoke _without fire._

10 Honesty is _the best policy._

C SENTENCE WORK

Complete the sentence so that it follows this one.

Rays from the sun can be harmful.

1 For example, _they can damage your skin._

2 Furthermore, _looking at the sun directly can harm your eyes._

3 Therefore, _it is important to use skin protection and wear sunglasses._

4 However, _don't let this spoil your summer fun._

Change the verb to include either **have** or **has**.

5 We ~~are holding~~ _have held_ talks with the shop's owner.

6 The plants ~~are beginning~~ _have begun_ to grow.

7 The wind ~~is doing~~ _has done_ a lot of damage.

8 Miss Hawkins ~~is teaching~~ _has taught_ us about plants.

PART C Focus
1–4: connectives to link ideas; sentences
5–8: verb tenses
9–10: use of semi-colons

Add three more items to the list.

9 The room was full of treasure: necklaces of glistening stones; rings with _the reddest of rubies; diamonds like pieces of ice; bags of gold coins._

10 He created a sumptuous feast: plates of roasted meats; steaming _bowls of fresh vegetables; warm, oven-fresh pastries; rich, creamy cakes._

X DEFINITIVE ANSWER   X SAMPLE ANSWER

A WARM-UP

Rewrite the sentence, changing the word order as you do so.

A figure appeared slowly, as the mist faded.

1 Slowly, as the mist faded, a figure appeared.

2 As the mist faded, a figure slowly appeared.

3 As the mist faded, a figure appeared slowly.

Write a word using these letters. The letters must be used in this order.

4 i l n   million

5 a f d   afford

6 x p n   expense

PART A Focus
1–3: ordering sentences for effect
4–6: visual spelling strategies
7–10: idioms

Add the missing animal.

7 Like water off a ___duck's___ back.

8 Let the ___cat___ out of the bag.

9 Give a ___dog___ a bad name.

10 Like a ___fish___ out of water.

B WORD WORK

Write sentences to show three different meanings of the word **just**.

1 It just happened.

2 It fitted just right.

3 It was a just verdict.

PART B Focus
1–3: homonyms
4: word structure
5–8: common tricky letter strings
9–10: common roots

4 Make four words by adding these affixes to the word **just**. Use each affix once only.

ad un in able ice ly ify

adjust, unjustly, injustice, justifiable

The same letter string is missing from all three words. Write it in.

5 offi _cial_   spe _cial_   benefi _cial_

6 vill _age_   mess _age_   dam _age_

7 import _ant_   eleph _ant_   const _ant_

8 do _dge_   ba _dge_   bu _dge_

Write three words that end like this.

9 **clude:** conclude, include, preclude

10 **gram:** anagram, diagram, telegram

C SENTENCE WORK

Rewrite the sentence in the passive form.

1 A security man guarded the painting. The painting was guarded by a security man.

2 Dr Gill organised the competition. The competition was organised by Dr Gill.

3 The mud ruined her shoes. Her shoes were ruined by the mud.

4 The Emperor saved the kingdom. The Kingdom was saved by the Emperor.

5 How is the passive version different? The receiver of the action is at the start of the sentence.

Continue the sentence to create different moods.

6 The room was lit by hundreds of tiny candles, sparkling like jewels.

7 The room was empty, with peeling wallpaper and discarded newspapers on the floor.

Punctuate the sentences. Use different punctuation marks in each one.

8 It seemed to me, or perhaps I imagined it, that the old man smiled.

9 If she fails—as I think she will—we must go on alone.

10 The planets orbit (travel round) the Sun.

PART C Focus
1–5: changing active to passive
6–7: word choice for effect; creating contrasting moods
8–10: parenthetic commas, brackets, dashes

A   WARM-UP

Use the words **car** and **tree** in

1 **an imperative:** Move that car from under the tree.

2 **a passive sentence:** The tree was damaged by the car.

3 **a complex sentence:** Heading towards a tree, the car suddenly swerved left.

4 **a rhyming couplet:**

Four cars parked under the tree

One car leaves – now there are three.

Make a word that ends and a word that starts with each letter string.

PART A Focus
1–3: varying sentence type
4: rhyme
5–7: visual spelling strategies; letter strings
8–10: rules for adding suffixes

5 lea ves → ves sel

6 geogra phy → phy sical

7 uni que → que stion

Underline the correct spelling.

8 busyest <u>busiest</u> busyist bussiest

9 <u>lonelier</u> lonlier lonelyer lonelyier

10 worryedly worridly <u>worriedly</u> worriedley

B   WORD WORK

1 Add the correct prefix.

PART B Focus
1–3: prefixes and their meanings
4–8: spelling rules and exceptions
9–10: meaning of idioms

post pre

<u>pre</u> caution   <u>post</u> script   <u>pre</u> view

Write the meaning of the prefix.

2 **pre:** before   **3** **post:** after

Add **able** or **ible**.

4 vis <u>ible</u>   detest <u>able</u>   resist <u>ible</u>

5 formid <u>able</u>   accept <u>able</u>   aud <u>ible</u>

Which two words above do **not** follow the usual **able/ible** pattern?

6 formidable   **7** resistible

8 What is the normal rule for adding **able** and **ible**?

'able' is added to a complete recognisable word and 'ible' to a stem.

Write a definition of the well-known saying.

9 **in the limelight:** the centre of attention

10 **to be given the sack:** to lose your job

C   SENTENCE WORK

Ravi waited by the door.

Rewrite the sentence, adding a subordinate clause to the

PART C Focus
1–3: adding subordinate clauses
4–7: text type; level of formality
8–10: use of colon

1 **beginning:** When it was time to leave, Ravi waited by the door.

2 **middle:** Ravi, who had seen exactly what happened, waited by the door.

3 **end:** Ravi waited by the door until the others had gone.

Write the text type that each sentence is taken from.

4 Mr Johal was born in 1948 in King's Norton, Birmingham.   biography

5 I was born in Hastings but my family moved to London when I was just two.   autobiography

6 Have just got in from college. What a day!   diary

7 Which is the most informal? the diary   Which is the most impersonal? the biography

Add a colon and complete the sentence.

8 He read the words on the sign: Harborough Hall.

9 Here is the address you need: 6 Park Street.

10 Evie read the opening words: 'Once upon a time there was a daydreamer named Flo.'

A   WARM-UP

Continue the sentence.

1   The clown danced even though _he_
    felt sad.

2   The clown danced as if _he were a_
    clockwork toy.

3   The clown danced whenever _the_
    music played.

Add a suffix to make the word into a verb.

4   crystal _lise_ (or lize)

5   beauty _ify_

6   critic _ise_ (or ize)

7   identity _fy_

Put the letters in order to make a word.

8   **g e a r u**   _argue_

9   **m y h e r**   _rhyme_

10 **r o o l u c**   _colour_

> **PART A Focus**
> **1–3:** connectives; subordinate clauses
> **4–7:** suffixes; word classes
> **8–10:** anagrams; visual spelling strategies

B   WORD WORK

Write an adverb to go with the definition.

1   _fiercely_   : with anger and aggression

2   _obviously_   : clearly

3   _usually_   : more often than not

Complete the word sum.

4   **gossip + ing =** _gossiping_

5   **quarrel + ing =** _quarrelling_

6   **shrub   + ery =** _shrubbery_

7   **stupid + ity =** _stupidity_

8   Which two words do **not** follow the spelling rule? Explain your answer.
    'gossiping' and 'stupidity', because
    you don't double the final consonant.

> **PART B Focus**
> **1–3:** adverbs; unstressed vowels
> **4–8:** spelling rules; exceptions
> **9–10:** subject-specific meanings

Write a definition.

9   **metre** (in maths): _a unit for_
    measuring length

10 **metre** (in poetry): _rhythm_

C   SENTENCE WORK

Rewrite the sentence with the subordinate clause at the beginning.

1   He stepped onto the stage despite his nerves.   _Despite his nerves, he stepped onto the stage._

2   The door opened as she stood there weeping.   _As she stood there weeping, the door opened._

3   What is the effect of reordering the clauses?   _It draws attention to the characters' feelings._

> **PART C Focus**
> **1–3:** effects of reordering clauses
> **4–6:** story genre; detail and word choice
> **7–10:** effects of punctuation

The door opened.

Rewrite the sentence, adding plenty of detail to match the story type.

4   **school story:** _The bell rang, the door opened and the class spilled out into the corridor._

5   **mystery:** _Slowly, the door opened and a figure moved silently into the room._

6   **sci-fi:** _Blake placed his palm on the ID pad and the lab door opened automatically._

How does the punctuation help to make the following more effective?

Stella is now my EX-best friend – officially.

7   **capital letters:** _used for emphasis._   8   **dash:** _to add a surprising comment._

Em' says it's my fault (but she would say that).

9   **brackets:** _to add a comment._   10   **apostrophes:** _for informal shortened forms._

A WARM-UP

Cross out the word that makes the phrase a cliché.
Write a more original simile.

1 as white as ~~snow~~
the first snowdrop of spring

2 as quiet as a ~~mouse~~
feather falling through the air

3 as deep as the ~~sea~~
ocean's unexplored depths

Write in full the word that the short form stands for.

4 ID — identity

5 fan — fanatic

6 ad — advertisement

7 demo — demonstration

Underline the hidden word.
Clue: it has at least four letters

8 s t r e <u>g i o n</u> t e

9 l e r p o <u>b e y c</u> e

10 w i <u>c h a o s</u> t l e

> **PART A Focus**
> **1–3:** writing similes
> **4–7:** spelling; short forms of longer words
> **8–10:** visual spelling strategies

B WORD WORK

Add the same suffix to all three words.

1 grace _ious_   thunder _ous_   env~y~ _ious_

2 effect _ive_   act _ive_   expense _ive_

3 music _al_   person _al_   nature _al_

4 Write the name of the class of words that you have made.
adjectives

> **PART B Focus**
> **1–4:** adding suffixes; word classes
> **5–6:** spelling strategies; unstressed vowels
> **7–10:** idioms

5 Add a short word to complete the longer word.

com _pan_ y   ske _let_ on

fat _ten_ ing   ve _get_ able

6 How does this help you to spell the words correctly?
It makes clear the unstressed vowel.

Add the same word to complete both idioms.

7 in _hot_ pursuit; red _hot_ favourite

8 the _heat_ is on; in the _heat_ of the moment

9 out _cold_ ; make the blood run _cold_

10 a _cool_ customer; keep your _cool_

C SENTENCE WORK

Complete the conditional sentence.

> **PART C Focus**
> **1–4:** conditional sentences
> **5–7:** summaries; connectives
> **8–10:** use of semi-colon

1 The sponsored walk will go ahead on Friday unless _it rains._

2 People would not drop litter if _there were more litterbins._

3 Martin will be able to come, provided that _he is over his cold._

4 They will be here soon, so long as _the traffic is not too bad._

Write a one-sentence summary of the story. Include a connective.

5 **Cinderella** _A young girl goes from rags to riches when she meets Prince Charming._

6 **Goldilocks** _A girl causes chaos in the bears' house, before running off on their return._

7 **Robin Hood** _A brave Sherwood Forest youth robs from the rich and gives to the poor – despite the Sheriff's best efforts._

Add a semi-colon.

8 There was no choice; we had to leave.

9 The house was empty; nothing stirred.

10 Don't interrupt; I haven't finished.

X DEFINITIVE ANSWER   X SAMPLE ANSWER

A   WARM-UP

Write a question-and-answer joke based on the homonym.

1 **trunk:** Where does an elephant pack?
In its trunk.

2 **wave:** Is the sea friendly?
Yes, it waves.

3 **watch:** What sort of dog ticks?
A watchdog.

Add the same short word to complete both longer words.

4 des _tin_ ation   ex _tin_ guish

5 cour _age_   man _age_

6 es _tab_ lish   s _tab_ le

7 be _lie_ ve   re _lie_ f

Add the missing letters.

Clue: story types

8 m y s t e r y

9 h u m o u r

10 a d v e n t u r e

PART A Focus
1–3: homonyms; word play
4–7: visual spelling strategies
8–10: spelling; story genre

B   WORD WORK

Add a word to complete each compound word.

1 _there_ fore

2 hence _forward_

3 _never_ theless

4 _more_ over

PART B Focus
1–4: formal connectives
5–7: spelling words with unstressed vowels
8–10: archaic language

5 Underline the unstressed vowels.

tel_e_graph   par_a_llel

mon_o_gram   mult_i_ply

6 Write the word root from the start of each word above.

tele, mono, para, multi

7 Why do root words help you to remember the correct spelling? Because the unstressed vowel is clear in the root.

Write a modern phrase that means the same.

8 **set forth:** set out

9 **yonder:** over there

10 **go thither:** go to that place

C   SENTENCE WORK

Rewrite the sentence in the passive form without mentioning the person or people responsible.

1 Jasper slew the dragon.   The dragon was slain.

2 The people sent a message.   A message was sent.

3 A servant had broken the mirror. The mirror had been broken.

4 The postman had delivered the letter. The letter had been delivered.

Complete the table with words and phrases used in formal and informal letters.

	formal	informal
5	domestic residence	home
6	Dear Sir or Madam	Hi!
7	in duplicate	with a copy

PART C Focus
1–4: passive forms
5–7: formal and informal language
8–10: using colons

Why has the colon been used?

8 There are three events: the sprint, long jump and high jump. To introduce a list.

9 The speech began very formally: "Ladies and gentlemen …" To introduce a quotation.

10 He knew he was late: it was past nine o'clock. To introduce a further explanation.

Section 2   Test 9

A   WARM-UP

The subject is **Mud**. Write sentences using each of these sound patterns.

1   alliteration: It's mucky and marvellous to mess in mud.

2   a rhyming couplet:
A muddy place is the best place to play
If I could, I'd stay there all day.

3   onomatopoeia: Slop, squelch go my wellies in the mud.

Underline the word that can **not** be a verb.

4   book float ring <u>planet</u> bat

5   pop spot <u>safe</u> snap bubble

6   light lead <u>year</u> note ferry

Solve the anagram.

7   hatcug: caught

8   netils: listen

9   paxilen: explain

10 nices: since

> **PART A Focus**
> **1–3:** word play; sound patterns
> **4–6:** word classes; meanings
> **7–10:** anagrams; visual spelling strategies

B   WORD WORK

1   Add the correct prefix. **sub anti extra**

anti freeze   anti dote   anti biotic

extra ordinary   extra vagant

sub merge   sub ordinate   sub terranean

Write the meaning of the prefix.

2   anti: against

3   extra: outside, beyond

4   sub: under, secondary

> **PART B Focus**
> **1–4:** prefixes; word meanings
> **5–6:** ch grapheme; less common sounds
> **7–10:** words that have changed meaning

5   Add the same grapheme to all the words.

ma ch inery   heada ch e

s ch olar   mis ch ief

6   Why is this grapheme tricky?
Because it makes different sounds that could also be made by other letters

Find the original meaning.

7   nice: ignorant, foolish

8   awful: awe-inspiring (full of awe)

9   terrific: causing terror

10 quick: alive, living

C   SENTENCE WORK

Rewrite the sentence as three separate sentences.

1   It was cold now that a fog had descended so the children shivered.
It was cold now. A fog had descended. The children shivered.

2   How does this change the impact? It creates a feeling of tension.

3   They raced to the door, which was locked, so there was no escape.
They raced to the door. It was locked. There was no escape.

4   How does this change the impact? It creates a feeling of urgency.

Complete the verb table.

5 **eat**	eats	eating	ate	eaten
6 **go**	goes	going	went	gone
7 **take**	takes	taking	took	taken
8 **blow**	blows	blowing	blew	blown

> **PART C Focus**
> **1–4:** short sentences for effect
> **5–8:** verb tenses
> **9–10:** varying sentence length; composing and punctuating sentences

9   Complete the sentence using fewer than 10 words: **Falling** to the ground, they lay still.

10 Complete the sentence using more than 20 words: **As Angie** walked across the playing field, she was glad of the soft breeze that cooled her face and calmed her troubled thoughts.

X **DEFINITIVE ANSWER**   X **SAMPLE ANSWER**

A   WARM-UP

Write four different sentences using these words only.

stood Jo holding the key there calmly

1   There stood Jo, calmly holding the key.

2   Holding the key calmly, there stood Jo.

3   There, calmly holding the key, stood Jo.

4   Jo stood there, holding the key calmly.

Write two words that follow the mnemonic.

5   I go home tonight   fight, might

6   I O U some   previous, glorious

Write the antonym.

7   **future**   past

8   **prefix**   suffix

9   **antonym**   synonym

10   **rhyming**   non-rhyming

> **PART A Focus**
> **1–4:** reordering for effect; commas
> **5–6:** spelling strategies; mnemonics
> **7–10:** technical vocabulary; antonyms

B   WORD WORK

Write the common root and its meaning.

1   astronaut astronomer asterisk
    'astro' means star.

2   monorail monocle monologue
    'mono' means single or one.

Add the correct suffix. Use each suffix once only.

3   **ful ment ly**
    move ment   wake ful   true ly

4   The odd one out is _____'truly'_____ , because you drop the 'e' when the suffix is added.

5   **able ist al**
    rehearse al   notice able   extreme ist

6   The odd one out is 'noticeable', because you keep the 'e' when adding a vowel suffix.

Write a simpler word with a similar meaning.

7   **endorse:**   support

8   **pursue:**   chase

9   **cease:**   stop

10   **commence:**   start

> **PART B Focus**
> **1–2:** meaning of roots
> **3–6:** rules for adding suffixes; exceptions
> **7–10:** formal vocabulary

C   SENTENCE WORK

Why has the writer used the passive?

1   The temperature was taken every hour. Because it doesn't matter who took it.

2   The poor man had been robbed. Because the robbed man is the most important.

3   The cloak had been cut to ribbons. Because it creates a mystery; we don't know who did it.

Use personification to complete the sentence.

4   The sun stretched out her fingers and touched the earth.

5   The sea played with the tiny boats, tossing them around.

6   The car groaned and spluttered, reluctant to be woken.

7   The river gurgled happily as it tumbled along.

Punctuate the sentence so that it sounds effective.

> **PART C Focus**
> **1–3:** effect of using passives
> **4–7:** personification
> **8–10:** punctuating sentences effectively

8   There, carved into the wood, was a number: 1004.

9   He ran, ran, ran – desperately, he ran.

10   It was an amazing sight – the spitting, hissing serpent, with its staring eyes and open jaws, quivering in the air.

Section 2 Test 11

A WARM-UP

Complete the sentence using a metaphor or personification.

1 Daisies _peep shyly from between the blades of grass._

2 An aeroplane _is a silver bird soaring into the sky._

3 Spring _lit up the world with her sunny smile._

Complete the table.

	adjective	noun	verb
4	real	reality	realise (ize)
5	visual	vision	visualise (ize)
6	confirmed	confirmation	confirm

Add the missing letters.

Clue: *sources of information*

7 d i c _t_ _i_ o n a _r_ _y_

8 b i b _l_ _i_ o g r a _p_ h y

9 e n c _y_ _c_ l o _p_ e d _i_ a

10 t h e s a _u_ r u s

PART A Focus
1–3: use of imagery
4–6: suffixes; word classes
7–10: spelling; technical vocabulary

B WORD WORK

1 Add the correct ending. **logy phobia athlon**

dec _athlon_   bio _logy_   tri _athlon_

hydro _phobia_ zoo _logy_   claustro _phobia_

Draw a line to join the root to its meaning.

2 athlon — fear of
3 logy — contest
4 phobia — the study of

PART B Focus
1–4: meaning of word roots
5–6: unstressed vowels
7–8: using root words to help spelling
9–10: meaning of proverbs

Add the missing vowels.

5 b e n _e_ f _i_ t   **6** s e p _a_ r _a_ t e

signal signature signpost unsigned

7 Underline the root.

8 Write the words in which the **g** is silent.

signpost, unsigned

Explain the meaning of the proverb.

9 Don't count your chickens before they are hatched. _Don't assume too soon that things will work out as you expect._

10 A fool and his riches are soon parted. _If you are foolish you will lose your money quickly._

C SENTENCE WORK

Make the sentence a conditional sentence.

1 I could borrow the bike _if I promised not to take it on the road._

2 He would be safe _so long as no-one saw him._

3 The team would score more goals _if they had a better striker._

4 You too can be a star player _if you have lessons._

Identify the text type.

story, information text, newspaper article

5 The crops have failed for the second year.   _newspaper article_

6 The crops shrivelled in the parched ground.   _story_

7 The ground becomes so dry that no crops can grow.   _information text_

Cross out the conjunction and replace it with a semi-colon.

8 Spring is nearly here; ~~so~~ buds will soon appear on the trees.

9 They whispered quickly; ~~because~~ there was not much time.

10 The light went out; ~~therefore~~ she could see nothing.

PART C Focus
1–4: forming conditional sentences
5–7: language features of texts
8–10: using semi-colons

X DEFINITIVE ANSWER   X SAMPLE ANSWER

Section 2 Test 12

A WARM-UP

Complete the proverb.

1 Too many cooks <u>spoil the broth.</u>

2 If at first you don't succeed,
<u>try, try and try again.</u>

Write a sentence to illustrate the proverb.

3 **Proverb 1:** <u>There were so many people</u>
<u>trying to organise the party that it</u>
<u>was a disaster.</u>

4 **Proverb 2:** <u>My dad failed his driving</u>
<u>test three times, but passed the</u>
<u>fourth time.</u>

Underline the word that is **not** linked by meaning.

5 bicycle binoculars <u>biography</u> biceps

6 decade decimal December <u>declare</u>

Underline the hidden word.
Clue: it has at least four letters

7 e s t <u>a c t i c</u> s e n

8 k i <u>c h e n c</u> e r d

9 m i <u>s h a l</u> f e r t

10 f r i <u>e l i k e l</u> i

PART A Focus
1–4: meaning of proverbs
5–6: word roots; meanings
7–10: visual spelling strategies

B WORD WORK

Add the missing letters.

1 e n v i r o <u>n</u> m e n t

2 g o v e r <u>n</u> m e n t

3 c u <u>p</u> b o a r d

4 r a s <u>p</u> b e r r y

PART B Focus
1–5: unstressed consonants
6–8: root words and affixes
9–10: older vocabulary

5 Explain why the words above are tricky to spell.
<u>The added letter is unstressed.</u>

Write two words formed by adding affixes to
the root word.

6 **music** <u>musical, musician</u>

7 **electric** <u>electrical, electrician</u>

8 **mobile** <u>automobile, mobility</u>

Write a modern word or phrase that means the same.

9 **pauper:** <u>beggar</u>

10 **coster:** <u>street seller</u>

C SENTENCE WORK

Complete the sentence.

1 Limping <u>painfully, she struggled home.</u>

2 Frightened <u>by the sudden noise, the frogs dived into the water.</u>

3 Leaping <u>bravely, they crossed the stream.</u>

4 Holding <u>the candle high, they could just make out the ceiling.</u>

We like skateboarding so <u>I think</u> a skateboard park would be <u>great</u>.

PART C Focus
1–4: constructing and punctuating sentences
5–7: personal and impersonal writing
8–10: using punctuation for effect

5 Underline the words that make this writing sound personal and informal.

6 Rewrite the sentence to make it sound impersonal.
<u>Many youngsters enjoy skateboarding so a skateboard park would be a useful facility.</u>

7 What is the purpose of this writing? <u>To make a suggestion and to persuade others.</u>

Punctuate the sentence and add capital letters where necessary.

8 She read the nameplate. Amy Miles. She knew the name. Where had she heard it?

9 A word of warning: if you are tempted to try this – don't!

10 That was when we realised. There was no going back – it was too late!

Schofield & Sims English Skills 5

Section 2 Writing task assessment sheet: Moving day

Name				Class/Set	
Teacher's name				Date	

Sentence structure and punctuation

	Always/often	Sometimes	Never
Varies sentence length and type for interest and authenticity (includes questions, exclamations, and short sentences for impact)			
Uses a variety of connectives to link clauses			
Time references varied; uses verbs accurately			
Shapes sentences (e.g., phrases, adverbs, clauses) for effect, interest and emphasis			
Sentence punctuation is correct			
Uses speech marks for direct quotes			
Uses commas (including parenthetic commas) to mark phrases and clauses			
Uses apostrophes correctly			
Uses sophisticated punctuation within sentences (e.g., dashes, brackets for inserted comments)			

Composition and effect

Uses questions and direct address to engage the reader			
Develops details about the events in linked paragraphs and sections			
Contrasting viewpoints established and maintained; persona of diary writers apparent			
Stylistic devices (e.g., detailed descriptions) are used to make writing entertaining			
Apt vocabulary choices add to impact and authenticity			
Content and detail are well chosen, and include personal comment and description of feelings			

Spelling

Familiar words spelt correctly			
Regular polysyllabic words spelt correctly			
Words with unstressed vowels spelt correctly			
Words with common letter strings or endings spelt correctly			
Roots, prefixes and suffixes spelt correctly			
Correct suffixes chosen (e.g., **ible/able**, **tion/sion**)			
Applies rules for adding suffixes and recognises common exceptions			
Applies other spelling rules (e.g., **ie**, **ei**) and recognises common exceptions			

Schofield & Sims English Skills 5

Section 2 Completed proofreading task: Tropical trees

Name		Class/Set
Teacher's name		Date

Factu~e~el di~i~escription *(a over e in Factuel, e over i in discription)*

Rainfor~i~est's pr~e~evide a very sp~e~etial ~in~invir~a~onment – a na~t~chural ha~b~bitat that is home to a v~a~erietty of tru~ell~y remark~i~ble plant's and an~i~amal's.

Wher~e~ever light reach~e~s the for~e~ist floor, e~x~gsotic ferns and herbs flu~o~rrish. H~H~igh above, the trees' branch~e~is form a can~n~opy of leafs *(ve)* and flow~e~ers, home to mil~lo~ians of insec~k~ts and an~i~amals. The trees pr~o~evide these cre~at~chures with a regul~a~er su~p~pley of food: fruits, nuts, seeds and poll~e~rn.

Poetic di~e~scription *(e over i in discription)*

Trees of dizz~y~eing h~i~eight tangel~e~ together, forming a secr~e~at gard~e~in not vis~i~able from bel~B~low. ~b~brightl~o~ey col~e~ured flow~e~ers entwhine the branch~e~is, with mouth~e~s open to the insist~e~ant rain.

O~w~nly tiny chinks of light and the drip~-~dro~p~ping of rain can p~e~irce the in~n~er darkn~e~iss of the rainfor~e~ist. Here, roots hang down like ropes da~n~ngling from an~c~shient bells.

Section 2 tasks summary

From: **English Skills 5 Answers** by Carol Matchett (ISBN 978 07217 1185 0). Copyright © Schofield & Sims Ltd, 2011. Published by Schofield & Sims Ltd, Dogley Mill, Fenay Bridge, Huddersfield HD8 0NQ, UK (www.schofieldandsims.co.uk). **This page may be photocopied for use within your school or institution only.**

Section 3 Test 1

A WARM-UP

Continue the sentence.

1 Jemma is happy as long as <u>she has her</u>
<u>music to listen to.</u>

2 Jemma is happy until <u>she has to tidy</u>
<u>her room.</u>

3 Jemma is happy while <u>Lucy is away</u>
<u>on holiday.</u>

4 Jemma is happy although <u>she is</u>
<u>sometimes homesick.</u>

Solve the anagram.

5 **helow:** <u>whole</u>

6 **athtug:** <u>taught</u>

7 **icento:** <u>notice</u>

8 **rathe:** <u>heart</u>

> **PART A Focus**
> **1–4:** using a range of conjunctions
> **5–8:** anagrams; visual spelling strategies
> **9–10:** word derivation

Explain the derivation.

9 **hyperlink** comes from <u>'hyper'</u>
<u>(meaning beyond normal) and 'link'</u>
<u>(meaning connection).</u>

10 **café** comes from <u>the French word for</u>
<u>coffee or coffee house.</u>

B WORD WORK

Write the correct spelling.

1 litracey <u>literacy</u>

2 mathmaticks <u>mathematics</u>

3 siense <u>science</u>

Write two words that start with the prefix.

4 **mal** <u>malfunction, malice</u>

5 **multi** <u>multiple, multitude</u>

6 Write the meaning of the prefix.

mal: <u>bad, badly</u>

multi: <u>many</u>

> **PART B Focus**
> **1–3:** spelling familiar words
> **4–6:** meaning of prefixes
> **7–10:** word meanings in different contexts

Write different definitions of each word.

7 **rap:** <u>a sharp tap</u>

8 **rap:** <u>a type of music</u>

9 **cricket:** <u>an insect like a grasshopper</u>

10 **cricket:** <u>a game played with bat and ball</u>

C SENTENCE WORK

Rewrite the sentence so that the information given in brackets is embedded within it.

1 The gerbil is best suited to life in the desert. (UK – popular pet) <u>The gerbil, a popular</u>
<u>pet in the UK, is best suited to life in the desert.</u>

2 Birds of prey include hawks and owls. (hawks hunt – day; owls hunt – night) <u>Birds of prey</u>
<u>include hawks, which hunt during the day, and owls, which hunt at night.</u>

3 Edward Jenner pioneered vaccination. (b. 1749; a doctor) <u>Edward Jenner (born in 1749)</u>
<u>was the first doctor to successfully introduce the practice of vaccination.</u>

What techniques has the writer of this advert used to persuade the reader to buy?

Get light on your feet with Flash trainers – truly awesome …

4 **sentence type:** <u>imperative</u>

5 **language:** <u>informal ('awesome')</u>

6 **word play:** <u>plays on the two meanings of the word 'light'</u>

7 **punctuation:** <u>uses a dash to add an informal comment</u>

Write a line of dialogue to open the traditional story.

8 **Red Riding Hood** <u>"Don't take that short cut," warned Red's mother.</u>

9 **Snow White** <u>"I love apples," said Snow White, taking a bite.</u>

10 **Aladdin** <u>"Put down that lamp and hurry up," came an impatient voice.</u>

> **PART C Focus**
> **1–3:** embedding information for economy
> **4–7:** language style and writing techniques
> **8–10:** punctuating dialogue

X DEFINITIVE ANSWER   X SAMPLE ANSWER

Section 3 Test 2

A WARM-UP

Write a sentence using these words.

spell caterpillar

1 **simple sentence:** I can spell 'caterpillar'.

2 **question:** Can you spell 'caterpillar'?

3 **compound sentence:** The wizard cast a spell and turned Jim into a caterpillar.

4 **complex sentence:** A caterpillar feeds for a spell of a few weeks before making a chrysalis.

Complete the words.

5   hap py → py ramid

6   ex it → it em

7   anim al → al most

8   lau gh → gh ost

> **PART A Focus**
> **1–4:** varying sentence type and length
> **5–8:** spelling strategies; letter strings
> **9–10:** word structure

Make three words.

9 **auto tele cue gram graph**
telegram, autograph, autocue

10 **med graph para ic al**
paramedic, medical, paragraph

B WORD WORK

Complete the word to go with the definition.
Use a dictionary to check the spelling.

1 ant ique   : very old

2 ant hology   : collection of poems or stories

3 ant agonism   : dislike; hostility

4 ant enna   : aerial; one of the feelers on an insect

5 These words are mixed up. Write them correctly.

webport helilung aquacam

heliport, webcam, aqualung

Write a more formal synonym.

6 **try**   endeavour

7 **watch over** supervise

8 **ask for**   request

9 **turn down**   decline

10 **go ahead**   proceed

> **PART B Focus**
> **1–4:** spelling strategies; use of dictionary
> **5:** word formation
> **6–10:** formal and informal word choice

C SENTENCE WORK

Complete the sentence.

1 Hiding her face behind a book, she crossed the room unnoticed.

2 Balanced precariously, he rescued the hat from the tree.

3 Peering over the banister, he could see the two figures arguing.

4 Surprised by the sudden attack, Dylan was unable to escape.

> **PART C Focus**
> **1–4:** varying sentence construction
> **5–7:** language features of texts
> **8–10:** use of brackets

What type of text is the sentence taken from?

5 Flour is mixed with water, yeast and salt.   explanation or information text

6 Mix the yeast and salt into the flour. Then add the water.   instructions (e.g., a recipe)

7 The salt and yeast were then added to the flour.   recount

Use brackets to add extra explanation or examples.

8 Icebergs are formed when glaciers (rivers of ice) meet the sea.

9 Bread, pasta (such as spaghetti and macaroni) and some cereals are made from wheat.

10 Different types of figurative language (such as similes and metaphors) are used to create a mood or feeling.

X DEFINITIVE ANSWER   X SAMPLE ANSWER

Section 3 Test 3

A WARM-UP

Write an advert for Sam's new range of soups using

1 **alliteration:** Savour Sam's soups soon.

2 **word play:** Sam's soups – they're souper!

3 **a rhetorical question:** Feeling the chill?

Want something warm and tasty?

4 **rhyme:** Have a hot glug from a mug.

Write a word using these letters. The letters must be used in this order.

5 **a b c** ambulance

6 **f g h** fight

7 **m n o** mnemonic

> **PART A Focus**
> **1–4:** word play; persuasive techniques
> **5–7:** visual spelling strategies
> **8–10:** prefixes; word structure

Write the prefix that can be added to all three words.

8 final colon circle — semi

9 natural structure human — super

10 light wake board — a

B WORD WORK

Add the same ending to all three words.

ary ery ory

1 direct ory   categ ory   fact ory

2 rot ary   volunt ary   tribut ary

3 myst ery   jewell ery   machin ery

4 Complete the word to go with the definition.

ball ad : a song or poem

ball et : a type of dance

ball ot : a vote

> **PART B Focus**
> **1–3:** tricky word endings
> **4–6:** word meanings and derivations
> **7:** word roots
> **8–10:** selecting homophones

Read the words you made in question 4.
Write the words that are derived from each meaning of the word **ball**. Use a dictionary to help you.

5 **ball:** a dance — ballad, ballet

6 **ball:** a round object — ballot

7 Write three words starting with the root **aero**.

aerobics, aerosol, aerodynamic

Underline the word in **bold** that is used correctly.

8 a weather **vein** / **vane** / **vain**

9 a ten-**story** / **storey** building

10 The tiger hunted its **pray** / **prey**.

C SENTENCE WORK

Rewrite the sentence in the passive form.

1 A sudden scream startled him. — He was startled by a sudden scream.

2 The swirling lights dazzled her. — She was dazzled by the swirling lights.

3 The man's strange clothing puzzled me. — I was puzzled by the man's strange clothing.

4 The sound of the sea calmed Ellie's mind. — Ellie's mind was calmed by the sound of the sea.

Add a word or phrase for emphasis.

5 This is absolutely vital.

6 This creature is now extremely rare.

7 The last , and most important, point is safety.

> **PART C Focus**
> **1–4:** use of the passive to alter focus
> **5–7:** techniques for emphasis
> **8–10:** use of colons

Add a colon and complete the sentence.

8 There are five vowels: 'a', 'e' 'i', 'o' and 'u'.

9 These are examples of conjunctions or joining words: when, although, until.

10 The room was now completely empty: everyone had gone home.

X DEFINITIVE ANSWER   X SAMPLE ANSWER

Section 3   Test 4

A   WARM-UP

Complete the warning using word play.

1 Be careful of lions _– they're always lyin'._

_____

2 Watch out for boars _– they are terrible_
      bores.

3 A cheetah _is sure to cheat ya!_

_____

Solve the anagram with a one-word answer.

4 **Wes ran:** _answer_

5 **Chloe coat:** _chocolate_

6 **Sid co:** _disco_

> PART A Focus
> **1–3:** word play
> **4–6:** anagrams; visual spelling strategies
> **7–10:** idioms

7 Write in the missing animal.

That's put the ___cat___ among the pigeons.

Write three other idioms featuring the same animal.

8 _Like a cat on hot bricks._

9 _It's raining cats and dogs._

10 _Has the cat got your tongue?_

B   WORD WORK

Check the spelling of the animal name.
Write the correct spelling.

1 pidgin   _pigeon_

2 sqirrul   _squirrel_

3 leperd   _leopard_

> PART B Focus
> **1–3:** checking spellings; using a dictionary
> **4–6:** suffixes; changing word class
> **7–10:** word meanings in different contexts

Use a suffix to make the noun into an adjective.

4 **triangle**   _triangular_

5 **hexagon**   _hexagonal_

6 **cylinder**   _cylindrical_

Write different definitions of each word.

7 **grate** (noun): _part of a fireplace_

8 **grate** (verb): _shave into small bits_

9 **hide** (noun):   _the skin of an animal_

10 **hide** (verb):   _Keep out of sight_

C   SENTENCE WORK

Reorder the sentence so that it focuses on the feelings of the character.

1 He walked on although he was scared.   _Although he was scared, he walked on._

2 They followed the others, as if in a trance.   _As if in a trance, they followed the others._

3 Ed crawled into the cave despite the pain.   _Despite the pain, Ed crawled into the cave._

4 He stood up with a tingle of excitement.   _With a tingle of excitement, he stood up._

> PART C Focus
> **1–4:** reordering sentences for effect
> **5–7:** language features; discussion texts
> **8–10:** commas to clarify meaning

5 Write three phrases that introduce one side of an argument.
Supporters argue; It is claimed that; Some people believe that

6 Write three phrases that introduce a different opinion.
Opponents point out; Critics of this view argue that; Those against argue

7 Write three connectives that introduce an opposing view.
However; On the other hand; In contrast

Add the missing commas.

8 Then there was the way she looked at me, unpleasantly, as if I were an insect.

9 When the beetroot is cool, press it through a sieve, collecting the juice in a bowl.

10 Smiling contentedly, Sarah sank into the armchair, glad to be home at last.

Section 3 Test 5

A WARM-UP

Write a sentence using these words.

goat socks

1 active: _The goat ate my socks._

2 passive: _My socks were eaten by the goat._

3 imperative: _Take the socks off the goat._

> **PART A Focus**
> 1–3: varying sentence type and form
> 4–7: spelling strategies
> 8–10: puns

Add a number to complete the word.

4 sen _ten_ ce   **6** w _eight_ less

5 l _one_ ly   **7** ne _two_ rk

Write a headline using a pun based on the homophones.

8 main/mane: _Safari park ready for mane event_

9 not/knot: _String is knot a problem for scouts_

10 aloud/allowed: _No girls aloud – girl-band concert cancelled_

B WORD WORK

Add the same ending to all three words. **cial tial**

1 essen _tial_   poten _tial_   torren _tial_

2 spe _cial_   artifi _cial_   finan _cial_

> **PART B Focus**
> 1–4: tricky endings
> 5–6: word roots
> 7–10: formal and informal word choice

Add the same ending to all three words.

3 popul _ar_   pill _ar_   regul _ar_

4 flav _our_   col _our_   hum _our_

Add a different root word to complete each of these space terms.

5 _uni_ verse   _super_ nova   _tele_ scope

6 _astro_ naut   _atmo(s)_ phere   _meteor_ ite

Write a more formal synonym to replace the word or phrase in **bold**.

7 Be **on your guard**.   _vigilant_

8 It was **okay**.   _satisfactory_

9 The amount was **not enough**.   _inadequate_

10 The place was **unfriendly**.   _inhospitable_

C SENTENCE WORK

Shorten the sentence by starting with the verb.

1 Although I was trembling with fear, I turned the key. Trembling _with fear, I turned the key._

2 Because she was running fast, she quickly caught up. _Running fast, she quickly caught up._

3 As he gathered his strength, he climbed higher. _Gathering his strength, he climbed higher._

4 Owing to the fact that I was encouraged by the applause, my confidence returned.
Encouraged by the applause, my confidence returned.

5 Underline the adjectives. **Each snowflake is individual and unique.**

6 What do the adjectives tell us about the design of snowflakes? _They are all different._

7 Underline the verbs. **As the bulldozers advance, all wildlife flees.**

8 Why has the writer chosen these verbs? _To make it sound as if the wildlife is under attack._

Add the commas, full stops and capital letters.

9 On the doorstep, Ayesha stopped. ̲S̲he must be too early. ̲T̲here was no sound coming
from inside, no music or sounds of laughter.

> **PART C Focus**
> 1–4: sentence variation for effect
> 5–8: word choice; effect
> 9–10: punctuation to clarify meaning: commas and full stops

10 Whales are mammals, not fish. ̲T̲hey are covered with skin, not scales.

[X] DEFINITIVE ANSWER   [X] SAMPLE ANSWER

Section 3   Test 6

A   WARM-UP

Write three different sentences using these words only.

came stomping the giant over the hill

1   Stomping over the hill came the giant.

2   The giant came stomping over the hill.

3   Over the hill came the stomping giant.

Complete the words.

4   marat hon → hon est

5   trans fer → fer ry

6   inter com → com municate

7   co mic → mic roscope

Underline the word that is wrongly spelt.

8   arguable   adorable   <u>agreable</u>

9   <u>dissbelief</u>   disservice   discourage

10   halves   <u>rooves</u>   thieves

> **PART A Focus**
> 1–3: varying word order
> 4–7: visual spelling strategies
> 8–10: spelling rules and exceptions

B   WORD WORK

Write the correct spelling of the library sign.

1   200 werld relijons and beleefs
    world religions and beliefs

2   400 Inglish and forern langwidges
    English and foreign languages

3   600 tecknolajy, mashines, invenshuns
    technology, machines, inventions

Write two words related to the word in **bold**.

4   **public**   publicity, publication

5   **memory**   memorable, memorial

6   **origin**   original, originate

Add the correct word.

larva lava

7   volcanic   lava

8   caterpillar   larva

> **PART B Focus**
> 1–3: correcting spellings
> 4–6: related meanings; spellings
> 7–10: homophones

symbols cymbals

9   I play the   cymbals.

10   There were   symbols   on the map.

C   SENTENCE WORK

Rewrite the sentence in the passive form to make it sound impersonal.

1   I sent a letter to the newspaper.   A letter was sent to the newspaper.

2   We will have to cancel the concert.   The concert will have to be cancelled.

3   We provide a choice of activities.   A choice of activities is provided.

4   I have taken steps to prevent this.   Steps have been taken to prevent this.

What narrative technique has the writer used to engage readers?

5   Hanif ran, Hasan ran, everyone ran.   repetition for effect

6   The path divided. Which way now?   question to make readers think

7   Well, what could I do?   direct address to readers

> **PART C Focus**
> 1–4: passives in impersonal writing
> 5–7: story-writing techniques
> 8–10: effective punctuation

Punctuate the text extract, adding capital letters if necessary.

8   Museum opening times: 10.00–6.00, last admission 5.00.
    Molly's cafe is open all day for snacks: sandwiches, rolls, cakes, tea and coffee.

9   Fanatical about football? Potty about the premiership? Try Striker, available NOW!

10   Force 9: roof tiles dislodged; damage to chimneys; branches blown off trees.

Section 3   Test 7

A   WARM-UP

Continue the sentence.

1 **active sentence:** The sword _pierced the_
knight's armour.

2 **passive sentence:** The sword _had_
been found.

3 **complex sentence:** The sword _glinted as_
Leo practised wielding it.

Add a short word to complete the longer word.

4 g_has_tly

5 o_bed_ient

6 a_band_oned

7 je_well_ery

> **PART A Focus**
> **1–3:** varying sentence types; structure
> **4–7:** spelling strategies
> **8–10:** exploring word roots

Complete the sentence.

8 **Archaeology** is the study of
ancient remains.

9 **Etymology** is the study of _words._

10 Underline the **ology** that is **not** a real word.

zoology meteorology <u>snowology</u> sociology

B   WORD WORK

Add the missing syllables.

1 dis / _guise_   **Clue:** *it hides who you are*

2 con / _so_ / nant   **Clue:** *not a vowel*

3 Add the same missing syllable to all three words.

gen / _er_ / al   av / _er_ / age   gen / _er_ / ous

4 How does saying syllables help you to spell?
It helps you to spot unstressed sounds.

Write two words related to the word in **bold**.

5 **refer**   _reference, referee_

6 **govern**   _government, governor_

> **PART B Focus**
> **1–4:** spelling strategies; use of syllables
> **5–6:** using root words to help spelling
> **7–10:** language from different times

Write a definition.

7 **schooner:** _sailing ship_

8 **buccaneer:** _pirate_

9 **doubloon:** _old Spanish coin_

10 If used in a story title, what would these words tell you about the setting?
That it is an historical story, set on a
pirate ship.

C   SENTENCE WORK

Complete the sentence with a statement of what might have happened.

1 If Jack had not climbed the beanstalk, _he might not have become rich._

2 If Cinderella had not lost her shoe, _the Prince might never have found her._

3 If Goldilocks had not run away, _the bears might have forgiven her._

4 If the boy had not cried 'Wolf!', _then people might have believed him._

Rewrite the sentence using more formal vocabulary.

5 We shouldn't wear jeans to school. _It is inappropriate to wear casual dress at school._

6 The centre helps old people. _The centre provides a valuable service for the elderly._

7 People want the councillors to rethink. _There is pressure on the council to reconsider._

8 We want money to make up for the mess. _We are seeking compensation for the damage._

9 Punctuate the information as **two** sentences, adding the capital letter where necessary.

On average, a person in the UK uses 150 litres of water a day._._ in parts of Africa,

each person has just ten litres a day.

> **PART C Focus**
> **1–4:** conditional sentences for supposition
> **5–8:** using formal language
> **9–10:** full stop, semi-colon

10 Punctuate it again as **one** sentence.

On average, a person in the UK uses 150 litres of water a day_;_ in parts of Africa,

each person has just ten litres a day.

38   X DEFINITIVE ANSWER   X SAMPLE ANSWER

Section 3   Test 8

A   WARM-UP

The subject is **Umbrellas**. Write a sentence using

1 **a rhyming couplet:**

Mr May's umbrella is grey

He carries it every single day.

2 **onomatopoeia:** Drip drop, plipperty plop

goes the rain on my umbrella.

3 **a simile:** Umbrellas open like a field of

colourful mushrooms.

Add one letter to make a different word.

4 scare   →   scarce

5 contact   →   contract

6 crate   →   create

> **PART A Focus**
> **1–3:** literary effects
> **4–6:** visual spelling strategies
> **7–10:** word origins

Draw a line to join the word in **bold** to its language of origin.

7 patio — Spanish

8 ski — Norwegian

9 solo — Italian

10 judo — Japanese

B   WORD WORK

Complete the word sum. Check the spelling carefully.

1 **humour** + ous = humorous

2 **fame** + ous = famous

3 **marvel** + ous = marvellous

> **PART B Focus**
> **1–3:** spelling rules; exceptions
> **4–7:** word roots and their meanings
> **8–10:** formal vocabulary

Write a definition.

4 **graphology:** the study of handwriting

5 **photophobia:** the fear of light

6 **transfigure:** to change in appearance

7 **micrometer:** device for measuring tiny objects

Complete the unfinished words in these formal signs.

8 All empl _oyees_ will be issued with a work per _mit_ .

9 Please en _sure_ that you pro vide a contact number for use in an em ergency .

10 Further details ava ilable on re quest .

C   SENTENCE WORK

Rearrange the sentence so that the subject comes at the end.

1 There was a huge bull right in front of me. There, right in front of me, was a huge bull.

2 There was the dog, staggering towards him, thin with hunger.

There, staggering towards him, thin with hunger, was the dog.

3 The giant beast slowly loomed out of a thin swirling mist.

Slowly, out of a thin swirling mist, loomed the giant beast.

> **PART C Focus**
> **1–3:** changing word order for effect
> **4–7:** selecting words for effect
> **8–10:** using dashes, colons, commas

A light drizzle began to fall, shrouding the street in greyness.

4 What mood has the writer created? A gloomy mood.

5 How has this been achieved? By the choice of words ('shrouding', 'greyness').

Complete the sentence to create a sense of

6 **calm:** The water rippled gently under the clear blue sky.

7 **tension:** The darkness silently crept around them, closing in on its prey.

Continue the sentence using either a comma, a dash or a colon.

8 A word of warning: dogs can bite.

9 Waving his fists, the baker ran after me.

10 Now he was frightened – more frightened than ever.

X DEFINITIVE ANSWER   X SAMPLE ANSWER

39

Section 3 Test 9

A WARM-UP

A tiger has escaped from the local zoo.

Rewrite the sentence as

1 **a headline:** Escaped tiger on loose

2 **a rhyming couplet:**

A tiger escaped from the local zoo

He's prowling the streets – what a to-do!

3 **a complex sentence:** A tiger escaped from the local zoo when his enclosure was left open accidentally.

Solve the anagram with a one-word answer.

4 **tears:** stare

5 **was here:** whereas

6 **I drew:** weird

> **PART A Focus**
> **1–3:** varying sentence type
> **4–6:** anagrams; visual spelling strategies
> **7–10:** word derivations

Write the day of the week that means

7 day of the Moon: Monday

8 day of Saturn: Saturday

9 day of the god Woden: Wednesday

10 day of the god Thor: Thursday

B WORD WORK

Write the correct spelling.

1 Shoping list: lettice, marjerine, rasberrys

Shopping list: lettuce, margarine, raspberries

2 Matereals: construksion card, addesive

Materials: construction card, adhesive

3 Eqipmunt: sissors, wire striper

Equipment: scissors, wire stripper

Write two words that start with the root.

> **PART B Focus**
> **1–3:** proofreading; checking spelling
> **4–6:** roots; linked words
> **7–10:** word meanings in different contexts

4 **cert** certain, certificate

5 **spect** spectator, spectacle

6 **quad** quadrilateral, quadrangle

Write different definitions of each word.

7 **mould** (in arts and crafts): to form a shape from a material

8 **mould** (in science): a kind of fungus

9 **scale** (in science): a small piece of skin on a snake or fish

10 **scale** (in geography): how distance is represented on a map

C SENTENCE WORK

Rewrite the sentence in the passive form, without mentioning who is responsible.

> **PART C Focus**
> **1–3:** use of passives to change focus
> **4–7:** writers' techniques; similes
> **8–10:** use of comma; semi-colon

1 Man's actions force some animals to find new habitats.

Some animals are forced to find new habitats.

2 Man hunted the dodo until it became extinct. The dodo was hunted to extinction.

3 People are cutting down large areas of forest. Large areas of forest are being cut down.

A penguin looks like a fat little waiter in evening dress.

4 Why does the writer use this simile? It gives a clear and appealing picture.

Write a simile of your own.

5 A hippopotamus has a body shaped like a barrel.

6 A diplodocus was as long as a swimming pool.

7 A peacock displays its tail like a carnival costume.

Put a tick if the sentence is correctly punctuated. Put a cross if it is not.

8 If commuters used public transport, the roads would be less crowded. ✓

9 Global warming is a huge concern, experts are worried about Earth's future. X

10 Write the incorrect sentence correctly.

Global warming is a huge concern; experts are worried about Earth's future.

Section 3   Test 10

A   WARM-UP

The subject is **The bee**. Write

1   an acrostic:

Busy buzzing
Everywhere
Endlessly

2   a rhyming couplet:

Buzzing wild, buzzing free
That's the life of a busy bee.

Write a word using these letters. The letters must be used in this order.

3   c i a   cinema

4   p l c   applicant

5   p t o   postpone

6   t f c   terrific

> **PART A Focus**
> **1–2:** poetic forms
> **3–6:** visual spelling strategies
> **7–10:** word play

Use word play to write a name for a

7   hairdresser: Headlines

8   fish and chip shop: The Jolly Fryer

9   flower shop: Busy Lizzy's

10   bakery: The Upper Crust

B   WORD WORK

Add the missing letter or letters.

Clue: is it single or double?

1 re_c_o_mm_end   **2** ne_c_e_ss_ary

3 Write a mnemonic for one of these words.

necessary: one Collar and two Sleeves

This is a made-up word. Write a definition.

4   autoathlon: a contest against yourself

5   triscopic: seeing three of everything

6   phobiometer: a device for measuring fear

What thou seest when thou dost wake,

Do it for thy true love take;

7 Underline the words which show that these lines were written long ago.

What do you notice about

the verbs?

> **PART B Focus**
> **1–3:** tricky spellings; mnemonics
> **4–6:** the meaning of word roots
> **7–10:** language from the past

8 A different verb ending is used ('st').

the pronouns?

9 'thy' is used instead of 'your'.

10 'thou' is used instead of 'you'.

C   SENTENCE WORK

Complete the sentence.

1 If we keep the plant in the cupboard, it will not grow green and strong.

2 If we all drove electric cars, less greenhouse gases would be produced.

3 A ban on cars in the town centre would help ease traffic congestion.

4 What is the purpose of sentences like these? They suggest ideas or theories.

Rewrite the sign using more formal language.

> **PART C Focus**
> **1–4:** conditional sentences
> **5–7:** formal language
> **8–10:** punctuating complex sentences

5 Sorry if the building work caused you problems.

We apologise for any inconvenience caused by the construction work.

6 You can't use your camera. The use of cameras is not permitted.

7 Be sure to have all your papers with you.

Please ensure that you have all the relevant documentation available.

Punctuate and continue the book blurb.

8 When Lenny the alien joins Class 6, strange things happen – especially to the teacher!

9 One stormy night, Josh finds shelter in a deserted barn – but is it really deserted?

10 Marcie, an orphan, lives with her gran in Victorian London, where she is very happy –

until her gran dies and she becomes homeless.

Section 3   Test 11

A   WARM-UP

Continue the sentence.

1 If you stand in the rain too long, _you may grow webbed feet._

2 If I were prime minister, _I would make every Friday a holiday._

3 If the sun forgot to rise, _then everyone would sleep all day._

Draw a line to join the dinosaur name to its meaning.

4 **megalosaurus** — great lizard
5 **triceratops** — three horned
6 **velociraptor** — fast plunderer

Underline the hidden word.
Clue: it has at least four letters

7 r i s t a **w a r e** r t h
8 p r e t h **a l s e** d i t e
9 t r a c i r c l e k t l e
10 n a d **g e n r e n** g e r d

PART A Focus
1–3: forming conditional sentences
4–6: word derivation and roots
7–10: visual spelling strategies

B   WORD WORK

Cross out the words that are wrongly spelt.
Write the correct spelling.

1 His ~~berthday~~ is ~~definately~~ in ~~Febuerry~~.
birthday, definitely, February

2 He ~~sined~~ the ~~holerday~~ form for the ~~secratery~~.
signed, holiday, secretary

3 I ~~prefered~~ the more ~~chalangeing clime~~.
preferred, challenging, climb

PART B Focus
1–3: proofreading; correcting spellings
4–6: rules for adding suffixes; exceptions
7–10: word meanings in different contexts

Add the same suffix to all three words.
ous ity ess

4 lion _ess_   god _dess_   prince _ess_
5 hazard _ous_   poison _ous_   envy _ious_
6 curious _ity_   generous _ity_   possible _ity_

Write different definitions of each word.

7 **font** (in RE): _vessel for baptisms_
8 **font** (in IT): _style of print_
9 **colon** (in science): _part of the digestive system_
10 **colon** (in literacy): _punctuation mark_

C   SENTENCE WORK

Rewrite each sentence twice. First make it shorter and more effective. Then make it longer and more effective.

Then they saw that Nina had vanished.

1 **shorter:** _Nina had vanished!_
2 **longer:** _As the mist cleared, they saw to their amazement that Nina had vanished._

They ran away as fast as they could.

3 **shorter:** _They ran._
4 **longer:** _Breathlessly, they ran away, their hearts racing, their lungs nearly bursting._

5 Tick the most effective story ending.

Then I woke up. It was all a dream. ___

We went home and had tea. ___

Peace returned to the planet – for a little while, at least. ✓

PART C Focus
1–4: lengthening and shortening for effect
5–6: engaging endings in narratives
7–10: comma; semi-colon

6 Explain your choice: _It adds a surprise to make the reader think._

Add a comma or a semi-colon.

7 The crowd parted; he stood alone.
8 As the fog lifted, the dawn began to break.
9 Racing past, she grabbed the sword.
10 It was frosty; I was glad of the hot drink.

42   X DEFINITIVE ANSWER   X SAMPLE ANSWER

Section 3 Test 12

A WARM-UP

Write a sentence using personification.

1 The volcano _belched out flames in fury._

2 Frost _stroked the land with icy fingers._

3 The machine _creaked reluctantly to life._

aqua auto hyper

mega scope scribe vision

> **PART A Focus**
> **1–3:** personification
> **4–7:** meaning of word roots
> **8–10:** spelling strategies; mnemonics

Make up four new words of your own, using these roots only. Then write a definition of each word.

4 _hypervision_ : _above/beyond normal_
vision

5 _autoscribe_ : _to write automatically_
without thinking

6 _megascope_ : _instrument for viewing_
large objects

7 _aquavision_ : _the ability to see_
under water

Write a mnemonic to help you spell

8 **people:** _oh please let's eat_

9 **length:** _Len goes to heaven_

10 **laugh:** _are u going home?_

B WORD WORK

Add the missing syllables.

1 vol / _un_ / _teer_ *Clue: unpaid worker*

2 c_om_ / p_ro_ / mi_se_ *Clue: an agreement*

3 ap / p_ro_ / _pri_ / _ate_ *Clue: suitable, fitting*

4 im / _me_ / _di_ / _ate_ / _ly_ *Clue: straightaway*

Write the word to go with the definition.
Use the root in **bold** to help you spell it.

5 _signature_ (noun):
the way you **sign** your name

6 _inactivity_ (noun):
a state of not being **active**

7 _extraordinary_ (adjective):
out of the **ordinary**

> **PART B Focus**
> **1–4:** spelling strategies; syllables
> **5–7:** using root words to aid spelling
> **8–10:** language of the past

These sentences are about a dance. Underline the words we do **not** use today. Write the words that we would use instead.

8 She <u>doth</u> but very softly go. _does_

9 <u>Tis</u> not fast; <u>tis</u> not slow. _It is_

10 <u>Foot it featly</u> here and there. _dance, neatly_

C SENTENCE WORK

We need money to keep the animal shelter open.

Express this idea in three different ways. Start each new sentence with the given word.

> **PART C Focus**
> **1–3:** constructing sentences in varied ways
> **4–7:** conveying meaning by implication
> **8–10:** punctuation to clarify meaning

1 Money _is needed to keep the animal shelter open._

2 If _you give money, it will be used to keep the animal shelter open._

3 Unless _money is made available, the animal shelter will have to close._

Rewrite the sentence so that it **shows** rather than **describes** the character's feelings.

4 Mum was angry. _Mum slammed the cupboard door, clattering the pans._

5 Ellen was scared. _Her hands shaking, Ellen lifted the latch._

6 Oliver was sad. _Oliver's bottom lip began to shake as he opened the letter._

7 Mr Jacks was happy. _Mr Jacks beamed at the class._

Correct the punctuation.

8 It's official! Banana's are the UK's favourite fruit, — we eat more of them than any other fruit.

9 Of course, keeping fit, is not just for players of sport; fitness is a goal for all.

10 There, hidden, below, was the treasure — the treasure that Jo had always dreamt of.

Schofield & Sims English Skills 5

Section 3 Writing task assessment sheet: Proposed road development

Name		Class/Set
Teacher's name		Date

Sentence structure and punctuation

	Always/often	Sometimes	Never
Varies sentence length (e.g., simple sentence for clarity, complex to explain; clauses embedded for economy of expression)			
Constructs sentences to express subtle distinctions of meaning (e.g., use of passives; conditionals)			
Uses appropriate and varied connectives			
Manipulates word order for emphasis and effect (e.g., placement of adverbials)			
Uses varied time references with verbs used accurately			
Maintains sentence punctuation			
Uses commas within complex sentences to mark boundaries and to clarify meaning			
Uses sophisticated formal punctuation marks (e.g., colon, semi-colon, brackets)			

Composition and effect

Effectively shapes the notice to include headline, opening statement, explanation of issue and details of meeting (e.g., time, place)			
Paragraphs have a clear focus and relationship between paragraphs is clear			
Maintains formal, balanced, impartial viewpoint (e.g., uses third person and makes generalised references)			
Uses stylistic techniques to capture interest (e.g., heading expressed as question)			
Formal language chosen is appropriate			
Ideas are tailored to the given reader (e.g., likely impact on local residents is explained)			

Spelling

Familiar words spelt correctly			
Words with unstressed vowels spelt correctly			
Words with familiar letter strings spelt correctly			
Endings correctly chosen (e.g., **ery**, **ary**, **ory**)			
Common roots, prefixes and suffixes spelt correctly			
Rules for adding endings correctly applied; common exceptions recognised			
General spelling rules applied; common exceptions recognised			

Schofield & Sims English Skills 5

Section 3 Completed proofreading task: Alone in a strange crowd

Name	Class/Set
Teacher's name	Date

It was quiet, incred(e)able. (O)one min(i)te I was in the liber(e)y, thum(b)ing thro(ugh)ow an old hist(o)ery book, and now... well, now w(e)re eg(x)sactly was I? The bookshel(ve)fs had van(n)ished, the comput(e)ers had van(n)ished, even the b(u)ilding had van(n)ished. (E)Evrything had just dis(s)apeared; I was al(l)one in a street full of strang(e)ers.

Nerv(o)usly, I shr(u)nk into the shad(o)ows, aw(a)re that pe(o)ple were ey(e)ing my cloth(e)s with a mix(t)ure of curi(o)usity and suspi(c)tion. I have to admit(t), a swe(a)tshirt and (j)geans did look a little out of pla(i)ce, (E)everyone el(l)se was dressed like (e)xtras from 'Oliver Twist'—all bus(t)sles and mag(c)itian(-)like top hat's. What was hap(p)enning(?). Was it someone's humo(u)rous little joke? I felt tota(l)y ab(b)andoned.

In confusi(o)n, and desp(e)rate to find something—or someone—familier, I set off in a trans(c)elike state, own(l)y narrow(l)ey avoid(d)ing a col(l)ision with a barrow and it's owner.

"W(a)tch where y(')(ou) goin(') mate," the barrow boy excl(a)med". "Just ar(r)i(v)ved from the country, have y(')(ou)? he added, in a q(u)aint but not unfr(i)endly tone.

Section 3 tasks summary

Full list of the Schofield & Sims English Skills books

Workbooks

For Key Stage 2:

English Skills 1	978 07217 1175 1
English Skills 2	978 07217 1176 8
English Skills 3	978 07217 1177 5
English Skills 4	978 07217 1178 2
English Skills 5	978 07217 1179 9
English Skills 6	978 07217 1180 5

The same workbooks, with covers designed for older users – at Key Stage 3 and beyond:

Essential English Skills 1	978 07217 1188 1
Essential English Skills 2	978 07217 1189 8
Essential English Skills 3	978 07217 1190 4
Essential English Skills 4	978 07217 1191 1
Essential English Skills 5	978 07217 1192 8
Essential English Skills 6	978 07217 1193 5

Answers

Suitable for use with both **English Skills** and **Essential English Skills**:

English Skills 1 Answers	978 07217 1181 2
English Skills 2 Answers	978 07217 1182 9
English Skills 3 Answers	978 07217 1183 6
English Skills 4 Answers	978 07217 1184 3
English Skills 5 Answers	978 07217 1185 0
English Skills 6 Answers	978 07217 1186 7

Teacher's Guide

The **Teacher's Guide** contains the **Workbook descriptors**, **Entry test** and many other useful items suitable for use with both **English Skills** and **Essential English Skills**:

English Skills Teacher's Guide	978 07217 1187 4

Also available

Mental Arithmetic (for Key Stage 2) and **Essential Mental Arithmetic** (for Key Stage 3 and beyond) are similar in format to **English Skills** and **Essential English Skills**, providing intensive maths practice.

For further information about both series, and for details of the **I can do** teaching method, which can be used with all the books mentioned on this page, visit **www.schofieldandsims.co.uk**